Professional Ethics.

AN ESSAY

ON

PROFESSIONAL ETHICS.

BY

GEORGE SHARSWOOD.

Id non eo tantum, quod si vis illa dicendi malitiam instruxerit, nihil sit publicis privatisque rebus perniciosius eloquentia: sed nos quoque ipsi, qui pro virile parte conferre aliquid ad facultatem dicendi conati sumus, pessime mereamur de rebus humanis, SI LATRONI COMPAREMUS HÆC ARMA, NON MILITI.

QUINCT. DE INST. OR.

Second Edition.

PHILADELPHIA:
T. & J. W. JOHNSON & CO.,
LAW BOOKSELLERS AND PUBLISHERS,
NO. 535 CHESTNUT STREET.
1860.

C. SHERMAN & SON, PRINTERS,

S. W. Cor. Seventh and Cherry Streets, Philadelphia.

TO

MY HONORED MASTER,

JOSEPH R. INGERSOLL, LL.D.,

INSCRIBED

AS A

TESTIMONY OF

RESPECT AND GRATITUDE.

PREFACE.

The following Essay was originally published under the title of "A Compend of Lectures on the Aims and Duties of the Profession of the Law, delivered before the Law Class of the University of Pennsylvania." A portion of it had been read by the author as an Introductory Lecture at the opening of the Fifth Session of the Law Department of that Institution, October 2d, 1854. The young gentlemen, alumni, and students of the school, who were present on that occasion, requested a copy for publication, in order that each of them might possess a memento of their connection with the Institution. The author preferred to publish the entire Compend than merely a part of it. He hesitated much in doing so, because the questions discussed are difficult, and opinions upon them variant, and he could scarcely hope that he had in every case succeeded in just discrimination. A review of the matter now, when a second edition has been called for, has suggested, however, no important change in the principles advanced, though a few additions have been made, some inaccuracies corrected, and an introduction upon the importance of the profession, in a public point of view, prefixed.

G. S.

INTRODUCTION.

The dignity and importance of the Profession of the Law, in a public point of view, can hardly be over-estimated. It is in its relation to society at large that it is proposed to consider it. This may be done by showing its influence upon legislation and jurisprudence. These are the right and left hands of government in carrying out the great purposes of society. By legislation is meant the making of law—its primary enactment or subsequent. alteration. Jurisprudence is the science of what the law is or means, and its practical application to cases as they arise. The province of legislation is *jus dare*—of jurisprudence, *jus dicere.* The latter is entirely in the hands of lawyers as a body—the former almost entirely.

Legislation is indeed a nobler work than even jurisprudence. It is the noblest work in which the intellectual powers of man can be engaged, as it resembles most nearly the work of the Deity. It is employed as well in determining what is right or wrong in itself—the due proportion of injuries and their remedies or punishments—as in enforcing what is useful and expedient. How wide the scope of such a work! The power of society over its individual members, or, in other words, sovereignty, which is practically vested in the legislature, is a type of the Divine power which rules the physical and moral universe. "There is one Lawgiver," says the Apostle James. Not that the Supreme Being is the sole universal lawgiver in the sense of a creator of law, whose will alone determines the boundaries of right and wrong. God is the creator of the beings who are the subjects of law. He is the author of law—the one lawgiver—in the same sense that he, who first discovered a plain figure, may be said to be the author of all theorems, which may be predicated of it. He who first called attention to the curious curve, made by a point in the periphery of a wheel as it turns on the ground, is in a certain sense the discoverer of all the truths, which may be mathematically demonstrated in respect to it.

Law in its true sense is not the work of mere will—not an act of intellectual caprice. It is a severe and necessary deduction from the relations of things. The Divine legislator sees and knows these relations perfectly. He can draw no wrong deduction from them. He can make no mistake. Whatever laws have certainly emanated from Him are certainly right. This is the sense in which it is true that "there is one Lawgiver:" all others but attempt the work; He alone is competent to perform it. There is no mathematical certainty in our reasoning on moral as there is on physical relations. We know that the three angles of a triangle are equal to two right angles with an assurance we can never have in regard to any moral truth whatever. The Divine law is a deduction necessarily and mathematically certain as much so as any truth in geometry. Human law can aim only at such a probable deduction as results from a finite and imperfect knowledge.

The system of law delivered by Moses to the Jews deserves, therefore, the most careful study at the hands of all who believe him to have been a divinely commissioned lawgiver. These laws were not intended for any other people than the Israelites; they were adapted to their circumstances, climate, country, neighbors, to the period of the world when they were promulgated, and during which they were to prevail. They were certainly not meant as a model for any other form of government, for any other people, or for any other time. Many laws are to be found there which are unnecessary and superfluous if applied elsewhere. Many actions, innocent in themselves, are prohibited. All the *mala prohibita* are not *mala in se*. But one thing is as clear as a sunbeam, and that is a very important light to the student of Ethics; if God was the author of these laws, nothing morally wrong was commanded or allowed by them. When it was said of the Jews through the prophet, "I gave them statutes which were not good," it cannot mean not morally good; laws which it would be sinful in them to obey. The word in the original is not the word appropriated in that language to right, conformity to rule, but to goodness in its most general sense. Good statutes mean wise and expedient statutes. By no process can the logical mind be brought to the conclusion that the perfectly wise and good lawgiver, in framing a code of laws for any people, would impose as a punishment "for the hardness of their hearts," a penalty, submission to which would itself be punishable as a sin against the law of nature. He might command or allow as such punishment what in itself was inexpedient and injurious to them, and which upon the promulgation of a new law repealing the old and prohibiting what it allowed, would become by the sanction of the same lawgiver thenceforth universally *malum prohibitum*. The authority of God as a lawgiver is certainly not confined to a mere declaration of what is right or wrong by the law of Nature.

There can be no merely arbitrary laws. It is necessary to bear in mind that we are now considering the province of the legislator, who ought to enact no law without an end. "Civil legislative power," says Rutherforth (B. II, c. vi, s. 10), "is not in the strict sense of the word an absolute power of restraining or altering the rights of the subjects: it is limited in its own nature to its proper objects, to those rights only in which the common good of the society or of its several parts requires some restraint or alteration. So that whenever we call the civil legislative power, either of society in general or of a particular legislative body within any society, an absolute legislative power, we can only mean that it has no external check upon it in fact; for all civil legislative power is in its own nature under an internal check of right: it is a power of restraining or altering the rights of the subjects for the purpose of advancing or securing the general good, and not of restraining or altering them for any purpose whatever, and much less for no purpose at all." There are, therefore, no arbitrary laws which fulfil the end of law. Doubtless the true objects of society and government may be mistaken by him who sets up to be law-maker, or if those objects are properly appreciated, the means for advancing them may be mistaken. It is not wonderful that in a matter which demands the highest wisdom, many should try and fail.

It becomes important to inquire what are the true ends of society and government? Man is a gregarious animal—a social being. He may exist in solitude, but he cannot enjoy life: he cannot perfect his nature. Those who have watched and studied closely the habits of those irrational animals, who live in communities, as the ant, the bee, and the beaver, have observed not only a settled system and subordination, but the existence of some wonderful faculty, like articulate speech, by which communication takes place from one to another; a power essential to order. Man, the highest social animal in the scale of earthly being, has also the noblest faculty of communication.

The final cause—the reason why man was made a social being—is that society was necessary to the perfection of his physical, intellectual, and moral powers, in order to give the fullest return to the labor of his hands and to secure the greatest advances in knowledge and wisdom. It is for no vain national power or glory, for no experimental abstraction, that governments are instituted among men. It is for man as an individual. It is to promote his development; and in that consists his true happiness. The proposition would be still more accurate were it said, society is constituted that men may be free—free to develop themselves—free to seek their own happiness, following their own instincts or conclusions. Without society—and government, which of course results from it—men would not be free. An individual in a state of isolation might defend himself from savage beasts, and more savage men, as long as his strength lasted, but when sickness or age came on, the product of the labor of his hands, accumulated by a wise foresight to meet such a contingency, would become the prey of the stronger. The comparatively weak-minded and ignorant would be constantly subject to the frauds of the more cunning.

It is enough to look at the effects of the division of employments and the invention of labor-saving machinery, to recognize the invaluable results of society in the development of wealth and power. In a state of isolation a man's entire time and strength would be needed for the supply of his physical wants. As men advance in knowledge and wisdom the standard of their mere physical wants is elevated. They demand more spacious and comfortable dwellings, more delicate viands and finer clothing.

> "Allow not nature more than nature needs,
> Man's life is cheap as beasts'."

It is not true that men would be morally better or happier, if their style of living were reduced to the greatest plainness consistent with bare comfort. Our taste in this respect, as for the fine arts, as it becomes more refined, becomes more susceptible of high enjoyment. When large fortunes are suddenly made by gambling, or what is equivalent thereto, then it is that baleful luxury is introduced—a style of living beyond the means of those who adopt it, and spreading through all classes. Taste, cultivated and enjoyed at the expense of morals, degrades and debases instead of purifying and elevating character. Men, who have accumulated wealth slowly by labor of mind or body, do not spend it extravagantly. If they use it liberally, that creates no envy in their poorer neighbor, no ruinous effort to equal what is recognized to be the due reward of industry and economy. The luxury, which corrupted and destroyed the republic of Rome, was the result of large fortunes suddenly acquired by the plunder of provinces, the conquests of unjust wars. The most fruitful source of it, in our own day, is what has been well termed *class legislation*—laws which either directly or indirectly are meant to favor particular classes of the community. They are supported by popular reasons and specious arguments, yet there is one test of the true character of such laws, an *experimentum crucis*, of which, in general, they cannot bear the application. Legislation, which requires or which will pay to be bored or bought, is unequal legislation; and therefore unwise and unjust. Bentham's rule, though false as the standard of right and wrong, is in general the true rule of practical legislation, the greatest good of the greatest number. It is expressed with the most force and accuracy by that master of the science, Bynkershoek; *Utilitas, utilitas, justi* PROPE *mater et æqui:* in which observe that the word *prope* is emphatic. Legislation for classes violates this plain rule of equal justice, and moreover does not, in the long run, benefit those for whom it is intended. The indirect evils upon society at large are even more injurious than those which are direct. Men are often thus poor to-day and rich to-morrow. The bubble, while it dances in the sunbeam, glitters with golden hues, though destined almost immediately to burst and be seen no more.

What government owes to society, and all it owes, is the impartial administration of equal and just laws. This produces security of life, of liberty, and of property. It has become a favorite maxim, that it is the duty of government to promote the happiness of the people. The phrase may be interpreted so as to mean well, but it is a very inaccurate and unhappy one. It is the inalienable right of men to pursue their *own* happiness; each man under such restraints of law as will leave every other man equally free to do the same. The true and only true object of government is to secure this right. The happiness of the people is the happiness of the individuals who compose the mass. Speaking now with reference to those objects only, which human laws can reach and influence, he is the happy man, who sees his condition in life constantly and gradually, though it may be slowly, improving. Let government keep its hands off—do nothing in the way of creating the subject-matter of speculation—and things naturally fall into this channel. There will be some speculators, as there will be some gamblers; but they will be few. The stock market is filled with fancies, which the government has manufactured and continues to manufacture to order. It is the duty of government to encourage the accumulation of the savings of industry. The best way to do so is to guard the strong box from the invasion of others, and not itself to invade it. Property has an especial claim to protection against the government itself. The power of taxation in the legislature is in fact a part of the *eminent domain;* a power that must necessarily be reposed in the discretion of every government to furnish the means of its own existence. One grievous invasion of property—and of course ultimately of labor, from whose accumulations all property grows—is by government itself, in the shape of taxation for objects not necessary for the common defence and general welfare. Men have a right not only to be well governed, but to be cheaply governed—as cheaply as is consistent with the due maintenance of that security, for which society was formed and government instituted. This, the sole legitimate end and object of law, is never to be lost sight of—security to men in the free enjoyment and development of their capacities for happiness—SECURITY—nothing less—but nothing more. To compel men to contribute of the earnings or accumulations of industry, their own or inherited, to objects beyond this, not within the legitimate sphere of legislation, to appropriate the money in the public treasury to such objects, is a perversion and abuse of the powers of government, little if anything short of legalized robbery. What is the true province of legislation, ought to be better understood. It is worth while to remark, that in every new and amended State constitution, the bill of rights spreads over a larger space; new as well as more stringent restrictions are placed upon legislation. There is no danger of this being carried too far; as Chancellor Kent appears to have apprehended that it might be. There is not much danger of erring upon the side of too little law. The world is notoriously too much governed. Legislators almost invariably aim at accomplishing too much. Representative democracies, so far from being exempt from this vice, are from their nature peculiarly liable to it. Annual legislatures—with generally two-thirds new members every year—increase the evil. The members fall into the common mistake, that their commission is to act, not to decide in the first place whether action is necessary. They would be blamed and ridiculed, if they adjourned without doing something important. Hence the annual volumes of our Acts of Assembly are fearfully growing in bulk. It is not merely of the extent of local legislation, the vast multiplication of charters for every imaginable purpose, or of the constantly recurring tampering with the most general subjects of interest, finance, revenue, banking, education, pauperism, &c., that there is reason to complain; but scarce a session of one of our legislatures passes without rash and ill-considered alterations in the civil code, vitally affecting private rights and relations. Such laws are frequently urged by men, having causes pending, who dare not boldly ask that a law should be made for their particular case, but who do not hesitate to impose upon the legislature by plausible arguments the adoption of some general rule, which by a retrospective construction, will have the same operation. It is a most monstrous practice, which lawyers are bound by the true spirit of their oath of office, and by a comprehensive view of their duty to the Constitution and laws, which they bear so large a part as well in making as administering, to discountenance and prevent. It is to be feared, that sometimes it is the counsel of the party who recommends and carefully frames the bill, which, when enacted into a law, is legislatively to decide the cause. It is time that a resort to such a measure should be regarded in public estimation as a flagrant case of professional infidelity and misconduct.

This brief sketch of the true province of legislation is enough to evince its vast importance. How great is the influence of the lawyers as a class upon legislation! Let any man look upon all that has been done in this department, and trace it to its sources. He will acknowledge that legislation, good or bad, springs from the Bar. There is in this country no class of lawyers confined to the mere business of the profession—no mere attorneys—no mere special pleaders—no mere solicitors in Chancery—no mere conveyancers. However more accurate and profound may be the learning of men, whose studies are thus limited to one particular branch, it is not to be regretted either on account of its influence on the science or the profession. The American lawyer, considering the compass of his varied duties, and the probable call which will be made on him especially to enter the halls of legislation, must be a Jurist. From the ranks of the Bar, more frequently than from any other profession, are men called to fill the highest public stations in the service of the country, at home and abroad. The American lawyer must thus extend his researches into all parts of the science, which has for its object human government and law:

he must study it in its grand outlines as well as in the filling up of details. He is as frequently called upon to inquire what the law ought to be as what it is. While a broad and marked line separates, and always ought to separate the departments of Legislation and Jurisprudence, it is a benefit to both that the same class of men should be engaged in both. Practice will thus be liberalized by theory, and theory restrained and corrected by practice. The mere abstractionist or *doctrinaire* would aim at the formation of a code of great simplicity: the practitioner sees in it the parent of uncertainty and injustice. Legal propositions cannot be framed with the certainty of mathematical theories. The most carefully studied language still leaves room for interpretation and construction. Time itself, which works such mighty changes in all things, produces a state of circumstances not in the mind of the lawgiver. The existing system, it may be, is an unwieldy, inconvenient structure, heavy and grotesque from the mixed character of its architecture outwardly, inwardly its space too much occupied and its inmates embarrassed by passages and circuities. The abstractionist would at once demolish it, and replace it by a light, commodious and airy dwelling, more symmetrical and chaste in its appearance, better fitted for the comfort and usefulness of its inhabitants. The practitioner, who has become familiar with it, who observes and admires that silent legislation of the people, which shows itself not on the pages of the statute book, and receives its recognition in courts of justice only after it has ceased to need even that to give it form and vitality, and who understands, therefore, how, with little inconvenience, it is made to accommodate itself to every change of condition, sits down to a careful calculation of the cost and risk of such wholesale change. History and practical experience, alike, suggest to him, that the structure is a castle as well as a dwelling, a place for security as well as comfort; that its foundations have been laid deeply on the solid rock—its masonry more firmly knit together by the time it has endured. Yet he will not deny that what can be done consistently with security ought to be done. It is worse than in vain to oppose all amendment. It will break down every artificial barrier that may be reared against it, if it be not quietly and wisely directed in those channels which it seeks at the least expense to security and stability. Surely it is not conceding too much to this spirit to admit, that laws should be composed in accurate but perspicuous language, without redundancy of words or involution of sentences; that the policy of public measures should not be wrapt up in the folds of State mystery; and that all legislation should be based upon the principle of leaving the greatest liberty of private judgment and action, consistent with public peace and private security. A blind attachment to principles of jurisprudence or rules of law because they are ancient, when the advancement of the useful arts, the new combinations of trade and business, and the influence of more rapid and general intercourse demand their repeal or modification, is as much to be deprecated as rash innovation and unceasing experiment. Indeed it scarcely ever fails to defeat its own end, and though it may retard for a while, renders the course of reform more destructive than it otherwise would have been. True conservatism is gradualism—the movement onward by slow, cautious, and firm steps—but still movement, and that onward. The world, neither physically, intellectually, nor morally, was made to stand still. As in her daily revolutions on her own axis as well as her annual orbit round the sun, she never returns precisely to the same point in space which she has ever before occupied, it would seem to be the lesson which the Great Author of all Being would most deeply impress upon mind as he has written it upon matter; "by ceaseless motion all that is subsists."

What has thus been very cursorily presented will evince that it is the province of legislation, by slow and cautious steps, to amend the laws, to render them more equal in their operation upon all classes, not favoring the rich more than the poor, nor one class of either more than another, providing an easy, cheap, and expeditious administration of justice by tribunals, whose learning and impartiality shall be so secured as to possess the confidence of the community, and by general rules for the regulation of conduct and the distribution of estates most conformed to the analogies of that system, which is familiar to the people in their common law.

Great as is the influence which the profession of the law can and does exercise upon the legislation of a country, the actual administration of law is entirely in their hands. To a large extent by private counsel, by the publication of works of research and learning, by arguments in courts of justice to assist those who are to determine what is the law, and to apply it to the facts, as well as in the actual exercise of judicature, this whole important province of government, which comes home so nearly to every man's fireside, is intrusted necessarily to lawyers.

In this country we live under the protection of written constitutions; not only so, but written constitutions, which have assumed to place limits upon the power of majorities, acting at least through their ordinary representatives. The construction of these constitutions, or constitutional law as it is termed, forms a very important branch of American jurisprudence. There have been, and are, in other countries, charters, written or unwritten—organic or fundamental laws—but without this distinguishing feature. The fundamental laws, thus established in point of fact, emanate from the government, and have no sanction beyond the oath of those intrusted with the administration of them, the force of public opinion, and the responsibility of the representative to his constituent. Our constitutions emanate not from the government, but the State, the society, the creator of the government; and are, therefore, in the strictest sense of the words, *leges legum*. The radical principle of our system is, that the act of the legislative body, beyond or contrary to the power confided to it by the Constitution, is a nullity, and absolutely void. The courts must so pronounce, and the executive must execute their judgments with the whole force of the State. Upon such a subject it is best to use the very language—the *ipsissima verba*—of John Marshall, as, at the same time, expressing the doctrine with the greatest force and perspicuity, and presenting, in the mere statement, the most convincing argument of its importance. "It is emphatically the province and duty of the judicial department to say what the law is. Those who apply the rule to particular cases, must, of necessity, expound and interpret that rule. If two laws conflict with each other, the courts must decide on the operation of each. So if a law be in opposition to the Constitution; if both the law and the Constitution apply to a particular case, so that the court must either decide that case conformably to the law, disregarding the Constitution, or conformably to the Constitution, disregarding the law: the court must determine which of these conflicting rules governs the case. This is of the very essence of judicial duty. If, then, the courts are to regard the Constitution, and the Constitution is superior to any ordinary act of the legislature, the Constitution, and not such ordinary act, must govern the case to which they both apply. Those, then, who controvert the principle that the Constitution is to be considered in court as a paramount law, are reduced to the necessity of maintaining that courts must close their eyes on the Constitution and see only the law. This doctrine would subvert the very foundation of all written constitutions. It would declare that an act, which, according to the principles and theory of our government, is entirely void, is yet, in practice, completely obligatory. It would declare that, if the legislature shall do what is expressly forbidden, such act, notwithstanding the express prohibition, is, in reality, effectual. It would be giving to the legislature a practical and real omnipotence with the same breath which professes to restrict their powers within narrow limits. It is prescribing limits, and declaring that those limits may be passed at pleasure." (Marbury *v.* Madison, 1 Cranch, 177.) More weighty words than these have never, speaking of human things, fallen from the lips of man: weighty in themselves from their own simple but eloquent conclusiveness—weightier still from their unspeakable importance, the immeasurable influence they have had, and, it is to be hoped, will ever continue to have, upon the destinies of the United States of America. The judiciary department, though originating nothing, but acting only when invoked by parties in the prosecution of their rights, is thus necessarily an important political branch of the government. That department spreads the broad and impregnable shield of its protection over the life, limbs, liberty, and property of the citizen, when invaded even by the will of the majority. Our Bills of Rights are, therefore, not mere enunciations of abstract principles, but solemn enactments by the people themselves, guarded by a sufficient sanction. They have not, perhaps, as yet, carried far enough their provisions for the security of property from the unjust action of government. The obligation of contracts has been declared sacred; the right of eminent domain restricted by the provision for compensation. Yet, even as to contracts, the legislature may still exercise dangerous powers over the remedy, short of taking it away entirely, and over the rules of evidence. As to eminent domain, they possess an undefined right to determine the time and manner of ascertaining the compensation. Our constitutions are frequently undergoing revision; and too much care cannot be exercised to strengthen our securities in this quarter. Personal liberty, trial by jury, the elective and other political franchises, liberty of conscience, of speech and of the press, are able to protect themselves in a great measure from their own democratic affinities. It is true, that there really is no difference between wresting from a man the few dollars, the products or savings of his industry for any period of time, and depriving him of his liberty, or chaining him to a log, to work for another during the same period. Property eminently stands in need of every parchment barrier, which has been or can be thrown around it. An eminent Judge in our own State once threw out the opinion that there existed in the Constitution no disaffirmance of the power of the legislature to take the property of an individual for *private uses* with or without compensation. "The clause," he argued, "by which it is declared that no man's property shall be taken or applied to *public* use, without compensation made, is a disabling, not an enabling one, and the right would have existed in full force without it." (Harvey *v.* Thomas, 10 Watts, 63.) Fortunately, the decision of the court in that case did not require a resort to that reasoning, and but little examination was sufficient to satisfy the mind that this *obiter dictum* was unsustained by either principle or authority. A power in the legislature to take the property of A. and give it to B. directly, would be of the very essence of despotism. When it is declared in the Bill of Rights that no man shall be deprived of his life, liberty, or property, unless by the judgment of his peers, or the law of the land, this phrase, "law of the land," does not mean merely an act of the legislature. If it did, every restriction upon the legislative department would be practically abrogated. By an authority as old as Lord Coke, in commenting upon these same words in *Magna Charta,* they are to be rendered "without due process of law: that is, by indictment or presentment of good and lawful men, when such deeds be done in due manner, or by writ original of the common law, without being brought into answer but by due process of the common law." (2 Inst. 50.) The American laws are numerous and uniform to the point (see 1 American Law Mag. 315); and the same eminent Judge, to whom reference has been made in a later case, declared his adhesion to the sound and true doctrine in the most emphatic language, without noticing his own previous *dictum* to the contrary. "It was deemed necessary," said he, "to insert a special provision in the Constitution to enable them (the legislature) to take private property even for public use, and on compensation made; but it was not deemed necessary to disable them specially in regard to taking the property of an individual, with or without compensation, in order to give it to another, not only because the general provision in the Bill of Rights was deemed sufficiently explicit for that, but because it was expected that no legislature would be so regardless of right as to attempt it. Were this reasonable expectation to be disappointed, it would become our plain and imperative duty to obey the immediate and paramount will of the people, expressed by their voices in the adoption of the Constitution, rather than the repugnant will of their delegates acting under a restricted but transcended authority." (Norman *v.* Heist, 5 W. & S. 171.)

Yet, while the right of private property cannot be thus directly invaded, its security against the acts of the legislature is not as perfect as it might and ought to be made. The legislature must be allowed a large discretion in judging what is a public use: on that pretext much may be brought within its sweep unjustly, and the courts, in the absence of a constitutional rule, would be embarrassed in defining its limits. Experience has shown that much power to do wrong lurks under grants by no means essential to the public good. Besides what has been before referred to, the assumption of judicial functions by the Legislature and the broad field of Chancery jurisdiction over trust estates, which it has been held that they may exercise immediately, if they see fit, instead of vesting them in appropriate tribunals, are fraught with serious danger. The proneness of bodies so constituted to disembarrass themselves of the ordinary rules of evidence, to act upon *ex parte* statements and testimony imperfectly authenticated, as well as the absence of all legal forms from their proceedings, and their numbers, among whom the responsibility of giving due attention to the case is divided, add to the peril. The power of legislating retrospectively has far too wide a scope; the constitutional inhibition of *ex post facto* laws having been construed to apply to criminal or penal cases merely, restraining the legislature from making that an offence which was not so at the time of its commission, or increasing the punishment annexed to it. The course of legislation in this country amply demonstrates the wisdom, and even necessity, of extending the same prohibition to civil cases. There is no particular or partial inconvenience, which could outweigh the general benefits of a provision that no law, public or private, should operate retrospectively upon past acts; that the judgment of the tribunals upon every case should be according to the law as it was at the time of the transaction, which the parties were bound to know, and in accordance with which they are to be presumed to have acted.

As well in the domain of public as of private law, the great fundamental principle for judge and counsellor ought to be, THAT AUTHORITY IS SACRED. There is no inconvenience so great, no private hardship so imperative, as to justify the application of a different rule to the resolution of a case, than the existing state of the law will warrant. "There is not a line from his pen," says Mr. Binney of Chief Justice Tilghman, "that trifles with the sacred deposit in his hands by claiming to fashion it according to a private opinion of what it ought to be. Judicial legislation he abhorred, I should rather say, *dreaded*, as an implication of his conscience. His first inquiry in every case was of the oracles of the law for their response; and when he obtained it, notwithstanding his clear perception of the justice of the cause, and his intense desire to reach it, if it was not the justice of the law, he dared not to administer it. He acted upon the sentiment of Lord Bacon, that it is the foulest injustice to remove landmarks, and that to corrupt the law is to poison the very fountains of justice. With a consciousness that to the errors of the science there are some limits, but none to the evils of a licentious invasion of it, he left it to our annual legislature to correct such defects in the system as time either created or exposed; and better foundation in the law can no man lay." It is not to be denied that there is some difficulty in stating with accuracy the limits of the rule *stare decisis*. One, or even more than one, recent precedent, especially when it relates to the application rather than to the establishment of a rule, is not of so binding a character that it must be followed, even though contrary to principles adjudged in older cases: but it is just as clear that when a decision has been long acquiesced in, when it has been applied in numerous cases, and become a landmark in the branch of the science to which it relates, when men have dealt and made contracts on the faith of it, whether it relates to the right of property itself, or to the evidence by which that right may be substantiated, though it may appear to us "flatly absurd and unjust," to overrule such a decision is an act of positive injustice, as well as a violation of law, and an usurpation by one branch of the government upon the powers of another. An example will illustrate this position. In the case of Walton *v.* Shelley (1 Term Rep. 296), in 1786, the King's Bench, Lord Mansfield, Chief Justice, decided that a person is not a competent witness to impeach a security which he has given, though he is not interested in the event of the suit, on the trial of which he is offered. In Jordaine *v.* Lashbrooke (7 Term Rep. 601), the same court, in 1798, under the presidency of Lord Kenyon, rightly overruled that decision. Now it so happens that Walton *v.* Shelley was recognized as authority and followed in Pennsylvania, in 1792, in Stille *v.* Lynch (2 Dall. 194), before it had been overruled in England: and though limited as it was understood to be in Bent *v.* Baker (3 Term Rep. 34), to negotiable paper (Pleasants *v.* Pemberton, 2 Dall. 196), it has never been varied from since that time, though it has frequently been admitted that Walton *v.* Shelley was properly overruled. It ought not now to be overruled in Pennsylvania. "After the decisions cited," says Judge Rogers, in Gest *v.* Espy (2 Watts, 268), "this cannot be considered an open question, nor do we think ourselves at liberty now to examine the foundations of the rule." Unfortunately our Supreme Court have not always put this sound and wise limitation upon their own power. In the case of Post *v.* Avery (5 W. & S. 509), they declared in regard to a rule of more than thirty years' standing, and confirmed by numerous cases, that they had "vainly hoped that the inconvenience of the rule would have attracted the attention of the legislature, *who alone are competent to abolish it;*" but as nothing was to be expected from that quarter, "they were driven by stress of necessity" to overrule a case expressly decided on the authority of the rule. (Hart *v.* Heilner, 3 Rawl. 407.) And two years afterwards, after having made the remarkable declaration that the legislature alone was competent to abolish the rule, they nevertheless pronounced it "exploded altogether." (McClelland *v.* Mahon, 1 Barr, 364.)

Lord Bacon says of retrospective laws: "*Cujus generis leges raro et magna cum cautione sunt adhibenda: neque enim placet Janus in legibus.*" Without any saving clause may the epithet and denunciation be applied to judicial laws. They are always *retrospective*, but worse on many accounts than *retrospective statutes.* Against the latter we have at least the security of the constitutional provision that prohibits the passage of any law, which impairs the obligation of a contract, executory or executed; and it has been well held that this prohibition applies to such an alteration of the law of evidence in force at the time the contract was made, as would practically destroy the contract itself by destroying the only means of enforcing it. There is no such constitutional provision against judicial legislation. It sweeps away a man's rights, vested, as he had reason to think, upon the firmest foundation, without affording him the shadow of redress. Nor could there, in the nature of things, be any such devised. When a court overrules a previous decision, it does not simply repeal it; it must pronounce it never to have been law. There is no instance on record, in which a court has instituted the inquiry, upon what grounds the suitor had relied in investing his property or making his contract, and relieved him from the disastrous consequences, not of his, but of their mistake, or the mistake of their predecessors. The man who, on the faith of Steele *v.* The Phœnix Ins. Co. (3 Binn. 306), decided in 1811, and treated as so well settled in itself and all its logical consequences, that in 1832 (Hart *v.* Heilner, 3 Rawle, 407) the Supreme Court declined to hear the counsel, who relied on its authority, invested his money in the purchase of a claim which could be proved only by the testimony of the assignor, found himself stripped of his property by a decision in 1845, the results of which were broader than even the legislature itself would have been competent to effect, or indeed the people themselves in their sovereign capacity, at least so long as the Constitution of the United States continues to be "the supreme law of the land, anything in the *constitution* and laws of any State to the contrary notwithstanding."

But judicial is much worse than legislative retrospection in another aspect. The act of Assembly, if carefully worded, is at least a certain rule. The act of the judicial legislature is invariably the precursor of uncertainty and confusion. Apply to it a test, which may be set down as unerring, never failing soon to discover the true metal from the base counterfeit: its effect upon litigation. A decision in conformity to established precedents is the mother of repose on that subject; but one that departs from them throws the professional mind at sea without chart or compass. The cautious counsellor will be compelled to say to his client that he cannot advise. One cause is the general uncertainty to which it leads. Men will persuade themselves easily, when it is their interest to be persuaded, that if one well-established rule has been overthrown, another, believed to be quite as wrong and perhaps not so well fortified by time and subsequent cases, may share the same fate. Shall counsel risk advising his client not to prosecute his claim or defence, when another bolder than he, may moot the point and conduct another cause resting upon the same question to a successful termination? The very foundations of confidence and security are shaken. The law becomes a lottery, in which every man feels disposed to try his chance. Another cause of this uncertainty is more particular. A court scarcely ever makes an open and direct overthrow of a deeply founded rule at one stroke. It requires repeated blows. It can be seen to be in danger, but not whether it is finally to fall. Hence it frequently happens that there is a sliding scale of cases; and when the final overthrow comes, it is very difficult to determine, whether any and which steps of the process remain. Shortly after the decision in Post *v.* Avery, the case of Fraley *v.* Bispham was tried in one of the inferior courts; in which the Judge, thinking that Post *v.* Avery, however the intention may have been disclaimed, did in fact overrule Steele *v.* The Phœnix, rejected as incompetent one of the nominal plaintiffs, a retiring partner, who upon dissolution had sold out for a price *bona fide* paid, all his interest in the firm to his copartners, who continued the business. A motion was made for a new trial, and before the rule came on to be heard, Patterson *v.* Reed (7 W. & S. 144) had appeared, and the court, on the authority of that case, which decided that an assignment must be colorable and made for the purpose of rendering the assignor a witness in order to exclude him, ordered a new trial. Before the case was again called for trial, the first volume of Barr's Reports had been published, in which the

Supreme Court said: "The time is come, when the doctrine of Steele *v.* The Phœnix Ins. Co. must be exploded altogether. The essential interests of justice demand that the decision in that case be no longer a precedent for anything whatever." (McClelland *v.* Mahon, 1 Barr, 364.) And the Judge before whom the cause was then tried had no other course left, but again to reject the witness, the very same thing on account of which a new trial had been ordered.

The case of Post *v.* Avery is a most striking illustration of judicial legislation and its mischievous results. It is usual to hear it excused on account of the unequal and unjust operation of the rule reversed, by which one party was heard but not the other, and the temptation it held out for the manufacture of false claims, to be supported by perjury. But it is to lose sight of the real question involved to raise such an issue: for, like the execution of a notorious culprit by the expeditious process of a mob and a lamp-post, instead of the formalities and delays of law and courts, it may be a very good thing for the community to have rid itself of the offender, but the way by which it was accomplished was a heavy blow at the very root of the tree of public and private security.

There is another decision of the Supreme Court of Pennsylvania, not so bold and avowed an act of judicial legislation as that just mentioned, but not less transparent, which may be cited as strongly illustrating the same consequences of uncertainty and litigation flowing from a disregard of the principle adverted to. From the year 1794, there had existed in Pennsylvania an act of Assembly limiting the lien of the debts of a decedent on his real estate, at first to seven, afterwards to five years. No question ever arose before the court in regard to it. Lien was considered to mean lien and not obligation: lands to be subject to execution for all debts of the owner prosecuted to judgment, and of course not barred by the Statute of Limitations; and the limitation of the lien merely intended for the protection of purchasers from the heirs or devisees or their lien creditors. Such was recognized to be the true meaning of the law in 1795 (Hannum *v.* Spear, 1 Yeats, 566), and so distinctly ruled in 1830 (Bruch *v.* Lantz, 2 Rawle, 392); yet on grounds palpably only relevant to what, in the opinion of the court, the law ought to be, it was held in 1832, in Kerper *v.* Hoch (1 Watts, 9), that the period named was a limitation not of the lien but of the debt itself, and available in favor of heirs and devisees, volunteers under the debtor and succeeding to his rights *cum onere.* As we have seen, but two cases are to be produced of litigation arising out of this law carried to the highest tribunal from 1794 to 1832. More than twenty cases are to be found reported since, in which that court has been called upon to draw distinctions and settle the precise extent of their own law. Thus a little complicated system has grown up on this construction of the act. A volume, indeed, might be written on Kerper *v.* Hoch and its satellites, when if the act had been let alone to speak for itself, and the prior decision followed, it would have been a simple and intelligible rule of action, until the legislature saw fit to alter it. It seems that this consideration pressed upon at least one of the judges, who joined in that decision; for in a subsequent case, when Kerper *v.* Hoch was cited, that Judge, with characteristic candor, interrupted the counsel with the remark: "We will abide by the rule, but it was erroneously decided." (Hocker's Appeal, 4 Barr, 498.)

This, then, is the legitimate province of Jurisprudence, *Stare super antiquas vias*, to maintain the ancient landmarks, to respect authority, to guard the integrity of the law as a science, that it may be a certain rule of decision, and promote that security of life, liberty, and property, which, as we have seen, is the great end of human society and government. Thus industry will receive its best encouragement; thus enterprise will be most surely stimulated; thus constant additions to capital by savings will be promoted; thus the living will be content in the feeling that their earnings are safely invested; and the dying be consoled with the reflection that the widow and orphan are left under the care and protection of a government, which administers impartial justice according to established laws.

With jurisprudence, lawyers have the most, nay all, to do. The opinion of the Bar will make itself heard and respected on the Bench. With sound views, their influence for good in this respect may well be said to be incalculable. It is indeed the noblest faculty of the profession to counsel the ignorant, defend the weak and oppressed, and to stand forth on all occasions as the bulwark of private rights against the assaults of power, even under the guise of law; but it has still other functions. It is its office to diffuse sound principles among the people, that they may intelligently exercise the controlling power placed in their hands, in the choice of their representatives in the Legislature and of Judges, in deciding, as they are often called upon to do, upon the most important changes in the Constitution, and above all in the formation of that public opinion which may be said in these times, almost without a figure, to be *ultimate sovereign.* Whether they seek them or are sought, lawyers, in point of fact, always have filled, in much the larger proportion over every other profession, the most important public posts. They will continue to do so, at least so long as the profession holds the high and well-merited place it now does in the public confidence.

PROFESSIONAL ETHICS.

There is, perhaps, no profession, after that of the sacred ministry, in which a high-toned morality is more imperatively necessary than that of the law. There is certainly, without any exception, no profession in which so many temptations beset the path to swerve from the line of strict integrity; in which so many delicate and difficult questions of duty are continually arising. There are pitfalls and man-traps at every step, and the mere youth, at the very outset of his career, needs often the prudence and self-denial, as well as the moral courage, which belong commonly to riper years. High moral principle is his only safe guide; the only torch to light his way amidst darkness and obstruction. It is like the spear of the guardian angel of Paradise:

> No falsehood can endure
> Touch of celestial temper, but returns
> Of force to its own likeness.

The object of this Essay is to arrive at some accurate and intelligible rules by which to guide and govern the conduct of professional life. It would not be a difficult task to declaim in general propositions—to erect a perfect standard and leave the practitioner to make his own application to particular cases. It is a difficult task, however, as it always is in practice, to determine the precise extent of a principle, so as to know when it is encountered and overcome by another—to weigh the respective force of duties which appear to come in conflict. In all the walks of life men have frequently to do this: in none so often as at the Bar.

The responsibilities, legal and moral, of the lawyer, arise from his relations to the court, to his professional brethren and to his client. It is in this order that it is proposed to consider and discuss the various topics which grow out of this subject.

The oath directed by law in this State to be administered upon the admission of an attorney to the bar, "to behave himself in the office of attorney according to the best of his learning and ability, and with all good fidelity, as well to the court as to the client; that he will use no falsehood, nor delay any man's cause for lucre or malice," presents a comprehensive summary of his duties as a practitioner.*

* This oath seems first to have been prescribed by the Act of Assembly, passed August 22d, 1752: "An act for regulating and establishing fees." (1 Smith's Laws, 218.) It has been copied into the revised Act of 14th April, 1834, s. 69 (Pamphlet Laws, 354), with the addition of the clause to "support the Constitution of the United States, and the Constitution of this Commonwealth." In England, by the Stat. 4 Henry IV, c. 18 (A. D. 1402), it was provided, "that all attorneys shall be examined by the Justices, and by their discretion, their names put in the roll, and they that be good and virtuous, and of good fame, shall be received, and sworn well and truly to serve in their offices,

Fidelity to the court, fidelity to the client, fidelity to the claims of truth and honor: these are the matters comprised in the oath of office.

It is an oath of office, and the practitioner, the incumbent of an office—an office in the administration of justice*—held by authority from those who represent in her tribunals the majesty of the commonwealth, a majesty truly more august than that of kings or emperors. It is an office, too, clothed with many privileges—privileges, some of which are conceded

and especially that they make no suit in a foreign country." The present oath or affirmation is, that he "will truly and honestly demean himself in the practice of an attorney, according to the best of his knowledge and ability." Stat. 2 Geo. II, c. 23 (A. D. 1729); Stat. 6 & 7 Vict. c. 73. The qualification of a sergeant-at-law, is given at large in 2 Inst. 213; and in the valuable old book, "The Mirror of Justices," chap. 2, sec. 5, it is said that "every countor is chargeable by the oath, that he shall do no wrong nor falsity, contrary to his knowledge, but shall plead for his client the best he can, according to his understanding."

* Hurst's case, 1 Levins, 72; 1 Sid. 94, 151; Raym. 56, 94; 1 Keb. 349, 354, 387.

to no other class or profession.* It is, therefore, that the legislature have seen fit to require

* See Austin's case, 5 Rawle, 203. "An attorney at law," says C. J. Gibson, "is an officer of the court. The terms of the oath, exacted of him at his admission to the bar, prove him to be so;" "you shall behave yourself in your *office* of attorney," &c. Again: it is declared in the Constitution, Article 1st, sec. 18 (Art. 1, sec. 19, of the amended Constitution of 1838), that "no member of Congress, or other person holding any *office* (except *attorney at law*, and in the militia), shall be a member of either House," &c., which is a direct constitutional recognition. Prior to the Act of 14th April, 1834, which expressly required from them an oath to support the Constitution of the United States and the Constitution of the Commonwealth of Pennsylvania, attorneys at law were invariably held to be within the provisions of Art. 6, sect. 3, of the Constitution of the United States, and of Art. 8, of the Constitution of Pennsylvania, requiring all officers, executive and judicial, to take the oath to support those constitutions respectively. In Wood's case (1 Hopkins, 6), solicitors in chancery were held to be officers, within the meaning of a similar clause in the Constitution of New York. "The admission of an attorney, solicitor, or counsellor," says the opinion in that case, "is a general appointment to conduct causes before the courts: this station, thus conferred by public authority, has its peculiar powers, privileges, and

that there should be added to the solemnity of the responsibility, which every man virtually

duties, and thus becomes an office in the administration of justice." Leigh's case (1 Munford, 468), in which it was held, that attorneys are not officers, within the meaning of the statute of Virginia, requiring all persons holding any office, or place, under the commonwealth, to take an oath against duelling, does not perhaps conflict with this view. The case of Byrne's Admr's *v.* Stewart's Admr's (3 Desaus. 478), may, however, be found upon examination somewhat at variance—not the decision itself, but the views expressed by Chancellor Watres in his opinion. The case simply decided what would seem unquestionable, that the legislature had a right to prohibit any public officer, judicial or otherwise, from practising as an attorney or solicitor. The Chancellor said, "He (a solicitor) can be considered in no other light than that of a private agent for the citizens of the country, who may employ him to do their legal business in the courts; and although the law requires of him certain qualifications, and he receives a license from the judges, yet his office is no more a public one, than would be any other profession or trade, which the legislature might choose to subject to similar regulations, and which is the practice in many other countries. It cannot be doubted, that a man's trade or profession is his property; and if a law should be passed avowedly for the purpose of restraining any member of this bar, who was not a public incurs when he enters upon the practice of his profession, the higher and more impressive sanction of an appeal to the Searcher of all Hearts.

officer, from exercising his profession, I should declare such law void." This is to assume high ground; but the idea that a man's profession or trade cannot be constitutionally interfered with by legislative enactments, seems scarcely tenable, and especially, so far as the profession of the law is concerned, in view of the absolute power with which every court is clothed, both as to the admission of their attorneys, and forejudging or striking them from the roll. Act of 14th April, 1834, s. 73 (Pamphlet Laws, 354). Courts of record and of general jurisdiction, are vested with exclusive power to regulate the conduct of their own officers, and in this respect their decisions are put on the same footing with that numerous class of cases, which is wisely confided to the legal discretion and judgment of the court, having jurisdiction over the subject-matter. Commonwealth *v.* The Judges, 5 Watts & Serg. 272; *Ex parte* Burr, 9 Wheat. 531; *Ex parte* Brown, 1 Howard (Miss.) Rep. 306; Perry *v.* State, 3 Iowa, 550; In the matter of Wills, 1 Mann, 392. "The power is one which ought to be exercised with great caution, but which is, we think, incidental to all courts, and necessary for the preservation of decorum and for the respectability of the profession." Marshall C. J. 9 Wheat. 531.

Fidelity to the court, requires outward respect in words and actions. The oath as it has been said, undoubtedly looks to nothing like allegiance to the person of the judge; unless in those cases where his person is so inseparable from his office, that an insult to the one, is an indignity to the other. In matters collateral to official duty, the judge is on a level with the members of the bar, as he is with his fellow-citizens; his title to distinction and respect resting on no other foundation, than his virtues and qualities as a man.* There are occasions, no doubt, when duty to the interests confided to the charge of the advocate demands firm and decided opposition to the views expressed or the course pursued by the court, nay, even manly and open remonstrance; but this duty may be faithfully performed, and yet that outward respect be preserved, which is here inculcated. Counsel should ever remember how necessary it is for the dignified and honorable administration of justice, upon which the dig-

* Per Gibson, C. J., in Austin's case, 5 Rawle, 204.

nity and honor of their profession entirely depend, that the courts and the members of the courts, should be regarded with respect by the suitors and people; that on all occasions of difficulty or danger to that department of government, they should have the good opinion and confidence of the public on their side. Good men of all parties prefer to live in a coun try, in which justice according to law is impartially administered. Counsel should bear in mind also the wearisomeness of a judge's office; how much he sees and hears in the course of a long session, to try his temper and patience. Lord Campbell has remarked that it is rather difficult for a judge altogether to escape the imputation of discourtesy if he properly values the public time; for one of his duties is to "render it disagreeable to counsel to talk nonsense." Respectful submission, nay, most frequently, even cheerful acquiescence in a decision, when, as is most generally the case, no good result to his cause can grow from any other course, is the part of true wisdom as well as civility. An exception may be noted to the opinion of the Bench, as easily in an agreeable and polite, as in a contemptuous and insulting manner. The excitement of the trial of a cause caused by the conflict of testimony, making often the probabilities of success to vibrate backwards and forwards with as much apparent uncertainty as the chances in a game of hazard, is no doubt often the reason and apology for apparent disrespect in manner and language; but let it be observed, that petulance in conflicts with the Bench, which renders the trial of causes disagreeable to all concerned, has most generally an injurious effect upon the interests of clients.

Indeed, it is highly important that the temper of an advocate should be always equal. He should most carefully aim to repress everything like excitability or irritability. When passion is allowed to prevail, the judgment is dethroned. Words are spoken, or things done, which the parties afterwards wish could be unsaid or undone. Equanimity and self-possession are qualities of unspeakable value. An anecdote may serve to illustrate this remark.

There was a gentleman of the Bar of Philadelphia, many years ago, who possessed these qualities in a very remarkable degree. He allowed nothing that occurred in a cause to disturb or surprise him. On an occasion in one of the neighboring counties, the circuit of which it was his custom to ride, he was trying a cause on a bond, when a witness for defendant was introduced, who testified that the defendant had taken the amount of the bond, which was quite a large sum, from his residence to that of the obligee, a distance of several miles, and paid him in silver in his presence. The evidence was totally unexpected; his clients were orphan children; all their fortune was staked on this case. The witness had not yet committed himself as to how the money was carried. Without any discomposure—without lifting his eyes or pen from paper—he made on the margin of his notes of trial a calculation of what that amount in silver would weigh; and when it came his turn to cross-examine, calmly proceeded to make the witness repeat his testimony step by step,—when, where, how, and how far the money was carried—and then asked him if he knew how much that sum of money weighed, and upon naming the amount, so confounded the witness, party, and counsel engaged for the defendant, that the defence was at once abandoned, and a verdict for the plaintiff rendered on the spot.*

Another plain duty of counsel is to present every thing in the cause to the court openly in the course of the public discharge of its duties. It is not often, indeed, that gentlemen of the Bar so far forget themselves as to attempt to exert privately an influence upon the judge, to seek private interviews, or take occasional opportunities of accidental or social meetings to make *ex parte* statements, or to endeavor to impress their views. They know that such conduct is wrong in itself, and has a tendency to impair confidence in the administration of justice, which ought not only to be pure but unsuspected. A judge will do right to avoid social intercourse with those who obtrude such

* The exact weight of one hundred silver dollars of the old coinage is 85·9375 ounces; of the new coinage, 80 ounces.

unwelcome matters upon his moments of relaxation. There is one thing, however, of which gentlemen of the Bar are not sufficiently careful,—to discourage and prohibit their clients from pursuing a similar course. The position of the judge in relation to a cause under such circumstances is very embarrassing, especially, as is often the case, if he hears a good deal about the matter before he discovers the nature of the business and object of the call upon him. Often the main purpose of such visits is not so much to plead the cause, as to show the judge who the party is—an acquaintance, perhaps—and thus, at least, to interest his feelings. Counsel should set their faces against all undue influences of the sort; they are unfaithful to the court, if they allow any improper means of the kind to be resorted to. *Judicem nec de obtinendo jure orari oportet nec de injuria exorari.* It may be in place to remark here that the counsel in a cause ought to avoid all unnecessary communication with the jurors before or during any trial in which he may be concerned. He should enforce the same duty upon his client. Any attempt by an attorney to influence a juror by arguments or otherwise, will, of course, if discovered and brought to the notice of the court, lead to expulsion or suspension from the Bar, according to the degree and quality of the offence. The freedom of the jury-box from extraneous influences is a matter of such vital moment in our system that the courts are bound to watch over it with jealous eyes. "It would be an injury to the administration of justice," says C. J. Tilghman, "not to declare that it is gross misbehavior for any person to speak with a juror, or for a juror to permit any person to speak with him, respecting the cause he is trying, at any time after he is summoned and before the verdict is delivered." "The words thus uttered," says Judge Hare, "by one of the best men and purest magistrates that ever filled the judicial office, must find an echo in every bosom. The principle which dictated them does not require the aid of argument or elucidation; it is native to the conscience, and will be apparent to all who consult the monitor in their own breast. The wrong is aggravated when the taint of personal interest mingles with it, as when committed by a party to the cause, but appears in the worst form when it is the act of attorneys or counsel, who are the sworn officers of the court, whose duty it is to act as guardians of the fountains of justice, and who are false to their charge when they defile or taint those waters, which they are pledged to keep pure and unpolluted. Such conduct in counsel is a gross breach of trust, for which a removal from the trust is but an inadequate punishment."*

There is another duty to the court, and that is, to support and maintain it in its proper province wherever it comes in conflict with the co-ordinate tribunal—the jury. The limits of these two provinces are settled with great accuracy; and even if a judge makes a mis-

* *Ex parte* Carter, 1 Philada. Rep. 507. Blaike's Lessee *v.* Chambers, 1 Serg. & Rawle, 169.

take, the only proper place to correct his error is in the superior tribunal,—the Court of Errors. It has been held in a multitude of cases, that verdicts against the charge of the court in point of law, will be set aside without limitation as to the number of times, and that without regard to the question whether the direction of the court in point of law was right or wrong. There is a technical reason, which makes this course in all cases imperative. The losing party, if the jury were allowed to decide the law for him, would be deprived of his exception, and of his unquestionable right to have the law of his case pronounced upon by the Supreme Court. *Ad questiones juris respondeant judices,—ad questiones facti juratores.* A disregard by the jury of the law, as laid down by the judge, is always therefore followed by additional and unnecessary delay and expense, and it is never an advantage to a party in the long run to obtain a verdict in opposition to the direction of the court.* It is best for

* Court and juries have their respective spheres assigned to them, within which each is to act and move, without

counsel to say in such cases, where nothing is left by the charge to the jury, that they do not

encroaching upon the jurisdiction or province of the other. In order, then, that jurors as well as others may know that the direction and decision of the court, on any question of law arising in the course of the trial of an issue of fact, is not to be disregarded, and that a verdict given against such direction, whatever it may be, can never avail anything, unless it be to occasion additional delay, trouble, and expense to the parties, as also to the public, the course of the court is to set the verdict aside, and to order a new trial. And a court, from whose decisions on questions of law, an appeal lies, by writ of error or otherwise, ought never to depart from this course; otherwise the party against whom the verdict is given loses the benefit of such appeal, and of having the question decided by the Appellate Court, which would be a most unjust and illegal deprivation of his right. Per Kennedy, J., in Flemming *v.* Marine Ins. Co. 4 Whart. 67. After two concurring verdicts against the direction of the court in point of law, a new trial will still be awarded. Commissioners of Berks County *v.* Ross, 3 Binn. 520. "Principles the most firmly established might be overturned, because a second jury were obstinate and rash enough to persevere in the errors of the first, in a matter confessed by all to be properly within the jurisdiction of the court; I mean the construction of the law arising from undisputed facts." Per Tilghman, C. J., Ibid. 524.

ask for a verdict. It has a fair, candid, and manly aspect towards court, jury, opposite party, and even client. Instances of counsel urging or endeavoring to persuade a jury to disregard the charge may sometimes occur, but they are exceedingly rare when there is good feeling between the Bench and the Bar, and when the members of the profession have just and enlightened views of their duty as well as interest.

It need hardly be added that a practitioner ought to be particularly cautious, in all his dealings with the court, to use no deceit, imposition, or evasion—to make no statements of facts which he does not know or believe to be true—to distinguish carefully what lies in his own knowledge from what he has merely derived from his instructions—to present no paper-books intentionally garbled. "Sir Matthew Hale abhorred," says his biographer, "those too com-

It is not necessary to refer to the numerous cases, both in the English and American courts, which accord with these principles. A judicious selection of the leading ones is to be found in the note to 1 Wharton's Troubat & Haly, 529. The text and the note are confined, of course, to civil cases.

mon faults of misrepresenting evidence, quoting precedents or books falsely, or asserting anything confidently by which ignorant juries and weak judges are too often wrought upon."* One such false step in a young lawyer will do him an injury in the opinion of the Bench and of his professional brethren, which it will take years to redeem, if indeed it ever can be entirely redeemed.

A very great part of a man's comfort, as well as of his success at the Bar, depends upon his relations with his professional brethren. With them he is in daily necessary intercourse, and he must have their respect and confidence, if he wishes to sail along in smooth waters. He cannot be too particular in keeping faithfully and liberally every promise or engagement he may make to them. One whose perfect truthfulness is even suspected by his brethren at the Bar has always an uneasy time of it. He will be constantly mortified by observing precautions taken with him which are not used with others. It is not only morally

* Burnet's Life of Sir Matthew Hale, 72.

wrong but dangerous to mislead an opponent, or put him on a wrong scent in regard to the case. It would be going too far to say that it is ever advisable to expose the weakness of a client's cause to an adversary, who may be unscrupulous in taking advantage of it; but it may be safely said, that he who sits down deliberately to plot a surprise upon his opponent, and which he knows can succeed only by its being a surprise, deserves to fall, and in all probability will fall, into the trap which his own hands have laid. "Whoso diggeth a pit," says the wise man, "shall fall therein, and he that rolleth a stone, it will return upon him." If he should succeed, he will have gained with his success not the admiration and esteem, but the distrust and dislike of one of his associates as long as he lives. He should never unnecessarily have a personal difficulty with a professional brother. He should neither give nor provoke insult. Nowhere more than at the Bar is that advice valuable:

> "Beware
> Of entrance to a quarrel; but being in,
> Bear it that the opposed may beware of thee."

There is one more caution to be given under this head. Let him shun most carefully the reputation of a sharp practitioner. Let him be liberal to the slips and oversights of his opponent wherever he can do so, and in plain cases not shelter himself behind the instructions of his client. The client has no right to require him to be illiberal—and he should throw up his brief sooner than do what revolts against his own sense of what is demanded by honor and propriety.

Nothing is more certain than that the practitioner will find, in the long run, the good opinion of his professional brethren of more importance than that of what is commonly called the public. The foundations of the reputation of every truly great lawyer will be discovered to have been laid here. Sooner or later, the real public—the business men of the community, who have important lawsuits, and are valuable clients—indorse the estimate of a man entertained by his associates of the Bar, unless indeed there be some glaring defect of popular qualities. The community know that they are better qualified to judge of legal attainments, that they have the best opportunity of judging, and that they are slow in forming a judgment. The good opinion and confidence of the members of the same profession, like the King's name on the field of battle, is "a tower of strength;" it is the title of legitimacy. The ambition to please the people, to captivate jurors, spectators, and loungers about the court room, may mislead a young man into pertness, flippancy, and impudence, things which often pass current for eloquence and ability with the masses; but the ambition to please the Bar can never mislead him. Their good graces are only to be gained by real learning, by the strictest integrity and honor, by a courteous demeanor, and by attention, accuracy and punctuality in the transaction of business.

The topic of fidelity to the client involves the most difficult questions in the consideration of the duty of a lawyer.

He is legally responsible to his client only for the want of ordinary care and ordinary skill. That constitutes gross negligence. It is extremely difficult to fix upon any rule which shall define what is negligence in a given case. The habits and practice of men are widely different in this regard. It has been laid down that if the ordinary and average degree of diligence and skill could be determined, it would furnish the true rule.* Though such be the

* An attorney is not answerable for every error or mistake; he ought not to be liable, in cases of reasonable doubt. Pitt *v.* Yalden, 4 Burrows, 2060. He shall be protected, when he acts with good faith, and to the best of his skill and knowledge. Gilbert *v.* Williams, 8 Mass. 57. The want of ordinary care and skill in such a person is gross negligence. Holmes *v.* Peck, 1 Rhode Island, Rep. 245; Cox *v.* Sullivan, 7 Georgia, 144; Pennington *v.* Yell, 6 Engl. 212. As between the client and the attorney, the responsibility of the latter is as great and as strict here as in any country when want of good faith or attention to the cause is alleged; but in the exercise of the discretionary power usually confided in this country, and especially when the client resides at a great distance, an attorney ought not to be held liable where he has acted honestly and in a way he thought was for the interest of his client. Lynch *v.* The Commonwealth, 16 Serg. & Rawle, 368; Stakely *v.* Robison, 10 Casey, 317. When, however, an

extent of legal liability, that of moral responsibility is wider. Entire devotion to the interest of the client, warm zeal in the maintenance and defence of his rights, and the exertion of his utmost learning and ability,—these are the higher points, which can only satisfy the truly conscientious practitioner.

But what are the limits of his duty when the

attorney disobeys the lawful instructions of his client, and a loss ensues, for that loss the attorney is responsible. Gilbert *v.* Williams, 8 Mass. 57. If the holder of a note place it in the hands of an attorney-at-law, with instructions to bring suit upon it, and the attorney, acting under the honest impression that he would best promote the interests of his client by not bringing suit immediately, omits to do so, and the money is afterwards lost by the insolvency of the maker, the attorney is liable in an action against him; and the measure of damages is what might have been recovered from the maker of the note, if suit had been brought when the note was placed in the hands of the attorney for collection. Cox *v.* Livingston, 2 Watts. & Serg. 103; Wilcox *v.* Plummer, 4 Peters, 172. But a client has no right to control his attorney in the due and orderly conduct of a suit, and it is his duty to do what the court would order to be done, though his client instruct him otherwise. Anon., 1 Wendell, 108.

legal demands or interests of his client conflict with his own sense of what is just and right? This is a problem by no means of easy solution.

That lawyers are as often the ministers of injustice as of justice is the common accusation in the mouth of gainsayers against the profession. It is said there must be a right and a wrong side to every lawsuit. In the majority of cases it must be apparent to the advocate, on which side is the justice of the cause; yet he will maintain, and often with the appearance of warmth and earnestness, that side which he must know to be unjust, and the success of which will be a wrong to the opposite party. Is he not then a participator in the injustice?

It may be answered in general:—

Every case is to be decided by the tribunal before which it is brought for adjudication upon the evidence, and upon the principles of law applicable to the facts as they appear upon the evidence. No court or jury are invested with any arbitrary discretion to determine a cause according to their mere notions of justice. Such a discretion vested in any body of men would constitute the most appalling of despotisms. Law, and justice according to law—this is the only secure principle upon which the controversies of men can be decided. It is better on the whole that a few particular cases of hardship and injustice, arising from defect of evidence or the unbending character of some strict rule of law, should be endured, than that general insecurity should pervade the community from the arbitrary discretion of the judge. It is this which has blighted the countries of the East as much as cruel laws or despotic executives. Thus the legislature has seen fit in certain cases to assign a limit to the period within which actions shall be brought; in order to urge men to vigilance, and to prevent stale claims from being suddenly revived against men whose vouchers are destroyed or whose witnesses are dead. It is true, *in foro conscientiæ*, a defendant, who knows that he honestly owes the debt sued for and that the delay has been caused by indulgence or confidence on the part of his creditor, ought not to plead the statute. But if he does plead it, the judgment of the court must be in his favor.

Now the lawyer is not merely the agent of the party; he is an officer of the court. The party has a right to have his case decided upon the law and the evidence, and to have every view presented to the minds of his judges, which can legitimately bear upon that question. This is the office which the advocate performs. He is not morally responsible for the act of the party in maintaining an unjust cause, nor for the error of the court, if they fall into error, in deciding it in his favor. The court or jury ought certainly to hear and weigh both sides; and the office of the counsel is to assist them by doing that, which the client in person, from want of learning, experience, and address, is unable to do in a proper manner. The lawyer, who refuses his professional assistance because in his judgment the case is unjust and indefensible, usurps the functions of both judge and jury.

As an answer to any sweeping objection made to the profession in general, the view thus presented may be quite satisfactory. It by no means follows, however, as a principle of private action for the advocate, that all causes are to be taken by him indiscriminately and conducted with a view to one single end, *success.* It is much to be feared, however, that the prevailing tone of professional ethics leads practically to this result. He has an undoubted right to refuse a retainer, and decline to be concerned in any cause, at his discretion. It is a discretion to be wisely and justly exercised. When he has once embarked in a case, he cannot retire from it without the consent of his client or the approbation of the court.* To

* An attorney is not compelled to appear for any one unless he takes his fee or backs the warrant. Anon., 1 Salk. 87. The attorney cannot determine the relation himself, to his client's detriment. Love *v.* Hall, 3 Yerger, 408. When a solicitor appointed by a party has acted as such, he cannot be displaced by the appointment of another, without an order of the court. Mumford *v.* Murray, 1 Hopkins, 369. After an attorney has entered his name upon the record, he cannot withdraw it without leave of the court; and until so withdrawn the service of a citation upon him in case of appeal is sufficient. United States *v.* Curry, 6 Howard, U. S. Rep. 106.

come before the court with a revelation of facts, damning to his client's case, as a ground for retiring from it, would be a plain breach of the confidence reposed in him, and the law would seal his lips.* How then is he to acquit him-

* A counsel, attorney, or solicitor, will in no case be permitted, even if he should be willing to do so, to divulge any matter which has been communicated to him in professional confidence. This is not his privilege, but the privilege of the client, and none but the client can waive it. Jenkinson *v.* The State, 5 Blackford, 465; Benjamin *v.* Coventry, 19 Wendell, 353; Parker *v.* Carter, 4 Munf. 273; Wilson *v.* Troup, 7 Johns. Ch. Rep. 25; Crosby *v.* Berger, 11 Paige, 377; Bank of Utica *v.* Mersereau, 3 Barbour Ch. Rep. 528; Aiken *v.* Kilburne, 27 Maine, 252; Crisler *v.* Garland, 11 Smedes & Marshall, 136; Chew *v.* The Farmers' Bank of Maryland, 2 Maryland Ch. Decis. 231. It will be found in some of these cases that though the counsel declined to be engaged for the client, yet the facts communicated were held confidential; the only exception recognized being where a purpose to perpetrate *in futuro* a felony or an action *malum in se* was disclosed. Bank of Utica *v.* Mersereau, 3 Barbour Ch. Rep. 377. In Moore *v.* Bray, 10 Barr, 519, it was held that communications of the object, for which an assignment of a mortgage was made, to a counsel concerned for the assignee, were privi-

self? Lord Brougham, in his justly celebrated defence of the Queen, went to very extravagant lengths upon this subject; no doubt he was led by the excitement of so great an occasion to say what cool reflection and sober reason certainly never can approve. "An advocate," said he, "in the discharge of his duty knows but one person in all the world, and that person is his client. To save that client by all means and expedients, and at all hazards and costs to other persons, and among them to himself, is his first and only duty; and in perform-

leged; although no question then arose as to the object of the assignment, and the counsel considered the communication in the light of a casual conversation. "The circle of protection," said Bell, J., "is not so narrow as to exclude communications a professional person may deem unimportant to the controversy, or the briefest and lightest talk the client may choose to indulge with his legal adviser, provided he regards him as such at the moment. To found a distinction on such a ground would be to measure the safety of the confiding party by the extent of his intelligence and knowledge, and to expose to betrayal those very anxieties, which prompt those in difficulty, to seek the ear of him in whom they trust in season and out of season."

ing this duty he must not regard the alarm, the torments, the destruction he may bring upon others. Separating the duty of a patriot from that of an advocate, he must go on reckless of consequences; though it should be his unhappy lot to involve his country in confusion."

On the other hand, and as illustrative of the practical difficulty, which this question presented to a man, with as nice a perception of moral duty as perhaps ever lived, it is said by Bishop Burnet, of Sir Matthew Hale: "If he saw a cause was unjust, he for a great while would not meddle further in it, but to give his advice that *it was so*; if the parties after that would go on, they were to seek another counsellor, for he would assist none in acts of injustice; if he found the cause doubtful or weak in point of law, he always advised his clients to agree their business. Yet afterwards he abated much of the scrupulosity he had about causes that appeared at first unjust, upon this occasion; there were two causes brought him, which by the ignorance of the party or their attorney, were so ill-represented to him that they seemed to be very bad; but he inquiring more narrowly into them, found they were really very good and just; so after this he slackened much of his former strictness of refusing to meddle in causes upon the ill circumstances that appeared in them at first."*

It may be delicate and dangerous ground to tread upon to undertake to descend to particulars upon such a subject. Every case must, to

* Burnet's Life of Hale, 1 Hale's Works, 59, 60. "He began," says Lord Campbell, "with the specious but impracticable rule of never pleading except on the right side, which would make the counsel to decide without knowing either facts or law, and would put an end to the administration of justice." 1 Lord Campbell's Lives of the Chief Justices, 412. There is the following curious note by Baxter in Burnet's Life of Hale. "And indeed Judge Hale would tell me that Bishop Usher was much prejudiced against lawyers because the worst causes find their advocates; but that he and Mr. Selden had convinced him of the reasons of it to his satisfaction; and that he did by acquaintance with them believe that there were as many honest men among lawyers, proportionably, as among any profession of men in England (not excepting bishops or divines)." 1 Hale's Works, 106.

a great degree, depend upon its own circumstances, known, peradventure, to the counsel alone; and it will often be hazardous to condemn either client or counsel upon what appears only. A hard plea—a sharp point—may subserve what is at bottom an honest claim, or just defence; though the evidence may not be within the power of the parties, which would make it manifest.

There are a few propositions, however, which appear to me to be sound in themselves, and calculated to solve this problem practically in the majority of cases: at least to assist the mind in coming to a safe conclusion *in foro conscientiæ*, in the discharge of professional duty.

There is a distinction to be made between the case of prosecution and defence for crimes; between appearing for a plaintiff in pursuit of an unjust claim, and for a defendant in resisting what appears to be a just one.

Every man, accused of an offence, has a constitutional right to a trial according to law: even if guilty, he ought not to be convicted and undergo punishment unless upon legal evidence; and with all the forms which have been devised for the security of life and liberty. These are the panoply of innocence when unjustly arraigned; and guilt cannot be deprived of it, without removing it from innocence. He is entitled, therefore, to the benefit of counsel to conduct his defence, to cross-examine the witnesses for the State, to scan, with legal knowledge, the forms of the proceeding against him, to present his defence in an intelligible shape, to suggest all those reasonable doubts which may arise from the evidence as to his guilt, and to see that if he is convicted, it is according to law. A circumstance the celebrated Lord Shaftesbury once so finely turned to his purpose must often happen to a prisoner at his trial. Attempting to speak on the bill for granting counsel to prisoners in cases of high treason, he was confounded, and for some time could not proceed, but recovering himself, he said, "What now happened to him would serve to fortify the arguments for the bill. If he innocent and pleading for others was daunted at the augustness of such an assembly, what must a man be who should plead before them for his life?"* The courts are in the habit of assigning counsel to prisoners who are destitute, and who request it; and counsel thus named by the court cannot decline the office.† It is not to be termed screening the guilty from punishment, for the advocate to exert all his ability, learning, and ingenuity, in such a defence, even if he should be perfectly assured in his own mind of the actual guilt of the prisoner.‡

* 2 Wynne's Eunomus, 557.

† "Although Serjeants have a monopoly of practice in the Common Pleas, they have a right to practice, and do practice, at this bar; and if we were to assign one of them as counsel, and he were to refuse to act, we should make bold to commit him to prison." Per C. J. Hale. 2 Campbell's Lives of the Chief Justices, 20; citing Freeman, 389; 2 Lev. 129; 3 Keble, 424, 439, 440.

‡ Let the circumstances against a prisoner be ever so atrocious, it is still the duty of the advocate to see that his client is convicted according to those rules and forms which the wisdom of the legislature have established, as the best protection of the liberty and security of the subject. Pro-

It is a different thing to engage as private counsel in a prosecution against a man whom he knows or believes to be innocent. Public prosecutions are carried on by a public officer, the Attorney-General, or those who act in his place; and it ought to be a clear case to induce gentlemen to engage on behalf of private interests or feelings, in such a prosecution. It ought never to be done against the counsel's own opinion of its merits. There is no call of professional duty to balance the scale, as there

fessor Christian's note to 4 Blackst. Com. 356. From the moment that any advocate can be permitted to say that he *will* or will *not* stand between the crown and the subject arraigned in the court where he daily sits to practise, from that moment the liberties of England are at an end. If the advocate refuses to defend from what *he may* think of the charge or of the defence, he assumes the character of the judge, nay, he assumes it before the hour of judgment; and in proportion to his rank and reputation, puts the heavy influence of perhaps a mistaken opinion into the scale against the accused, in whose favor the benevolent principle of English law makes all presumptions, and which commands the very judge to be his counsel. Lord Erskine, 6 Campbell's Lives of the Chancellors, 361.

is in the case of a defendant. It is in every case but an act of courtesy in the Attorney-General to allow private counsel to take part for the Commonwealth; such a favor ought not to be asked, unless in a cause believed to be manifestly just. The same remarks apply to mere assistance in preparing such a cause for trial out of court, by getting ready and arranging the evidence and other matters connected with it: as the Commonwealth has its own officers, it may well, in general, be left to them. There is no obligation on an attorney to minister to the bad passions of his client; it is but rarely that a criminal prosecution is pursued for a valuable private end, the restoration of goods, the maintenance of the good name of the prosecutor, or closing the mouth of a man who has perjured himself in a court of justice. The office of Attorney-General is a public trust, which involves in the discharge of it, the exertion of an almost boundless discretion, by an officer who stands as impartial as a judge. "The professional assistant, with the regular deputy, exercises not his own discretion, but that of the Attorney-General, whose *locum tenens* at sufferance, he is; and he consequently does so under the obligation of the official oath."* On the other hand, if it were considered that a lawyer was bound or even had a right to refuse to undertake the defence of a man because he thought him guilty, if the rule were universally adopted, the effect would be to deprive a defendant, in such cases, of the benefit of counsel altogether.

The same course of remark applies to civil causes. A defendant has a legal right to require that the plaintiff's demand against him should be proved and proceeded with according to law. If it were thrown upon the parties themselves, there would be a very great inequality between them, according to their intelligence, education, and experience, respectively. Indeed, it is one of the most striking advantages of having a learned profession, who engage as a business in representing parties in courts of justice, that men are thus brought

* Per Gibson, C. J., in Rush *v.* Cavenaugh, 2 Barr, 189.

nearer to a condition of equality, that causes are tried and decided upon their merits, and do not depend upon the personal characters and qualifications of the immediate parties.* Thus, too, if a suit be instituted against a man to recover damages for a tort, the defendant has a right to all the ingenuity and eloquence he can command in his defence, that even if he has committed a wrong, the amount of the damages may not exceed what the plaintiff is justly entitled to recover. But the claim of a plaintiff stands upon a somewhat different footing. Counsel have an undoubted right, and are in duty bound, to refuse to be concerned for a plaintiff in the legal pursuit of a demand, which offends his sense of what is just and right. The courts are open to the party in person to prosecute his own claim, and plead

* "There are many who know not how to defend their causes in judgment, and there are many who do, and therefore pleaders are necessary; so that that which the plaintiffs or actors cannot or know not how to do by themselves, they may do by their serjeants, attorneys, or friends." Mirr. of Justices, ch. 2, sec. v.

his own cause; and although he ought to examine and be well satisfied before he refuses to a suitor the benefit of his professional skill and learning, yet it would be on his part an immoral act to afford that assistance, when his conscience told him that the client was aiming to perpetrate a wrong through the means of some advantage the law may have afforded him. "It is a popular but gross mistake," says the late Chief Justice Gibson, "to suppose that a lawyer owes no fidelity to any one except his client, and that the latter is the keeper of his professional conscience. He is expressly bound by his official oath to behave himself, in his office of attorney, with all fidelity to the court as well as the client; and he violates it when he consciously presses for an unjust judgment, much more so when he presses for the conviction of an innocent man. . . . . The high and honorable office of a counsel would be degraded to that of a mercenary, were he compelled to do the biddings of his client against the dictates of his conscience."* The sentiment has been expressed in flowing numbers by our great commentator, Sir William Blackstone:—

"To Virtue and her friends a friend,
Still may my voice the weak defend:
Ne'er may my prostituted tongue
Protect the oppressor in his wrong;
Nor wrest the spirit of the laws,
To sanctify the villain's cause."

Another proposition which may be advanced upon this subject is, that there may and ought to be a difference made in the mode of conducting a defence against what is believed to be a righteous, and what is believed to be an unrighteous claim. A defence in the former case should be conducted upon the most liberal principles. When he is contending against

* Rush *v.* Cavenaugh, 2 Barr, 189. If the client in any suit furnishes his attorney with a plea which the attorney finds to be false, so that he cannot plead it for *the sake of* his conscience, the attorney may plead in this case, *quod non fuit veraciter informatus*, and in so doing he does his duty. Jenkins, 52.

the claim of one, who is seeking, as he believes, through the forms of law, to do his client an injury, the advocate may justifiably avail himself of every honorable ground to defeat him. He may begin at once by declaring to his opponent or his professional adviser, that he holds him at arm's length, and he may keep him so during the whole contest. He may fall back upon the instructions of his client, and refuse to yield any legal vantage ground, which may have been gained through the ignorance or inadvertence of his opponent. Counsel, however, may and even ought to refuse to act under instructions from a client to defeat what he believes to be an honest and just claim, by insisting upon the slips of the opposite party, by sharp practice, or special pleading—in short, by any other means than a fair trial on the merits in open court. There is no professional duty, no virtual engagement with the client, which compels an advocate to resort to such measures, to secure success in any cause, just or unjust; and when so instructed, if he believes it to be intended to gain an unrighteous object, he ought to throw up the cause, and retire from all connection with it, rather than thus be a participator in other men's sins.

Moreover, no counsel can with propriety and a good conscience express to court or jury his belief in the justice of his client's cause, contrary to the fact. Indeed, the occasions are very rare in which he ought to throw the weight of his own private opinion into the scales in favor of the side he has espoused. If that opinion has been formed on a statement of facts not in evidence, it ought not to be heard,—it would be illegal and improper in the tribunal to allow any force whatever to it;—if on the evidence only, it is enough to show from that the legal and moral grounds on which such opinion rests. Some very sound and judicious observations have been made by Mr. Whewell in a recent work on the Elements of Moral and Political Science, which deserve to be quoted at length;—

"Some moralists," says he, "have ranked with the cases in which convention supersedes the general rule of truth, an advocate asserting the justice, or his belief in the justice, of his client's cause. Those who contend for such indulgence argue that the profession is an instrument for the administration of justice: he is to do all he can for his client: the application of laws is a matter of great complexity and difficulty: that the right administration of them in doubtful cases is best provided for if the arguments on each side are urged with the utmost force. The advocate is not the judge.

"This may be all well, if the advocate let it be so understood. But if in pleading he assert his belief that his cause is just when he believes it unjust, he offends against truth, as any other man would do who in like manner made a like assertion.

"Every man, when he advocates a case in which morality is concerned, has an influence upon his hearers, which arises from the belief that he shares the moral sentiments of all mankind. This influence of his supposed morality is one of his possessions, which, like all his possessions, he is bound to use for moral ends. If he mix up his character as an advocate with his character as a moral agent, using his moral influence for the advocate's purpose, he acts immorally. He makes the moral rule subordinate to the professional rule. He sells to his client not only his skill and learning, but himself. He makes it the supreme object of his life to be not a good man, but a successful lawyer.

"There belong to him, moreover, moral ends which regard his profession; namely, to make it an institution fitted to promote morality. To raise and purify the character of the profession, so that it may answer the ends of justice without requiring insincerity in the advocate, is a proper end for a good man who is a lawyer; a purpose on which he may well and worthily employ his efforts and influence."*

Nothing need be added to enforce what has been so well said. The remark, however, may

* Whewell's Elements of Moral and Political Science, vol. 1, p. 257.

be permitted, that the expression of private opinion as to the merits of a controversy often puts the counsel at fearful odds. A young man, unknown to the court or the jury, is trying his first case against a veteran of standing and character: what will the asseveration of the former weigh against that of the latter? In proportion, then, to the age, experience, maturity of judgment, and professional character of the man, who falsely endeavors to impress the court and jury with the opinion of his confidence in the justice of his case, in that proportion is there danger that injury will be done and wrong inflicted—in that proportion is there moral delinquency in him who resorts to it.

Much interest was excited some years ago in England, by the circumstances attending the defence of Courvoisier, indicted for the murder of Lord William Russell. The crime was one of great atrocity. It came out after his conviction, that during the trial he had confessed his guilt to his counsel, of whom the eminent barrister Charles Phillips, Esq., was one. Mr.

Phillips was accused of having endeavored, notwithstanding this confession, to fasten suspicion on the other servants in the house, to induce the belief that the police had conspired with them to manufacture evidence against the prisoner, and to impress the jury with his own personal belief in the innocence of his client. How far these accusations were just in point of fact was the subject of lively discussion in the newspapers and periodicals of the time.*

The language of counsel, on such occasions, during the excitement of the trial, in the fervor of an address to the jury, is not to be calmly and nicely scanned in the printed report. The testimony of such a witness as Baron Parke, at the time and on the spot,—he, too, aware of the exact position of Mr. Phillips—

*Law Magazine, February, 1850, May, 1854. Law Review, February, 1850. Several articles on the subject, taken from the English press, are to be found in Littell's Living Age, vol. 24, pp. 179, 230, 306. I have added, in an appendix, Mr. Phillips's vindication of himself from these charges, in his correspondence with his friend Mr. Warren, preceded by a brief statement of the case.

and that confirmed by Chief Justice Tindal, is conclusive. To charge him with *acting falsehood*, that is, with presenting the case as it appeared upon the testimony, earnestly and confidently, means that he did not do that, which would have been worse than retiring from his post.

The non-professional, as well as professional public in England, however, agreed in saying that he would not have been justified in withdrawing from the case: he was still bound to defend the accused upon the evidence; though a knowledge of his guilt, from whatever source derived, might and ought materially to influence the mode of the defence. No right-minded man, professional or otherwise, will contend that it would have been right in him to have lent himself to a defence, which might have ended, had it been successful, in bringing down an unjust suspicion upon an innocent person; or even to stand up and falsely pretend a confidence in the truth and justice of his cause, which he did not feel. But there were those on this side of the Atlantic, who demurred to the conclusion, that an advocate is under a moral obligation to maintain the defence of a man who has admitted to him his guilt. Men have been known, however, under the influence of some delusion, to confess themselves guilty of crimes which they had not committed: and hence, to decline acting as counsel in such a case, is a dangerous refinement in morals.* Nothing seems plainer than the proposition, that a person accused of a crime is to be tried and convicted, if convicted at all, *upon evidence*, and *whether guilty or not guilty*, if the evidence is insufficient to convict him, he has *a legal right* to be acquitted. The

* The civil law will not allow a man to be convicted on his bare confession, not corroborated by evidence of his guilt; because there may be circumstances which may induce an innocent man to accuse himself. Bowyer's Commentaries, 355, note. Upon a simple and plain confession, the court hath nothing to do but to award judgment; but it is usually very backward in receiving and recording such confession out of tenderness to the life of the subject; and will generally advise the prisoner to retract it and plead to the indictment. 4 Blackst. Comm. 329. 2 Hale, P. C. 225.

tribunal that convicts without sufficient evidence may decide according to the fact; but the next jury, acting on the same principle, may condemn an innocent man. If this be so, is not the prisoner in every case entitled to have the evidence carefully sifted, the weak points of the prosecution exposed, the reasonable doubts presented which should weigh in his favor? And what offence to truth or morality does his advocate commit in discharging that duty to the best of his learning and ability? What apology can he make for throwing up his brief? The truth he cannot disclose; the law seals his lips as to what has thus been communicated to him in confidence by his client. He has no alternative, then, but to perform his duty. It is his duty, however, as an advocate merely, as Baron Parke has well expressed it, to use ALL FAIR ARGUMENTS ARISING ON THE EVIDENCE. Beyond that, he is not bound to go in any case; in a case in which he is satisfied in his own mind of the guilt of the accused, he is not justified in going.

Under all circumstances, the utmost candor

should be used towards the client. This is imperatively demanded alike by considerations of duty and interest. It is much better for a man occasionally to lose a good client, than to fail in so plain a matter. It is nothing but selfishness that can operate upon a lawyer when consulted to conceal from the party his candid opinion of the merits, and the probable result. It is fair that he should know it; for he may not choose to employ a man whose views may operate to check his resorting to all lawful means to effect success. Besides, most men, when they consult an attorney, wish a candid opinion; it is what they ask and pay for. It is true, that it is often very hard to persuade a man that he has not the best side of a lawsuit: his interest blinds his judgment: his passion will not allow him to reflect calmly, and give due weight to opposing considerations. There are many persons who will go from lawyer to lawyer with a case, until they find one who is willing to express an opinion which tallies with their own. Such a client the lawyer, who acts firmly upon the principle to which I have adverted, will now and then lose; but even such an one, when finally unsuccessful, as the great probability is that he will be, when he comes to sit down and calculate all that he has lost in time, money, and character, by acting contrary to the advice first given, will revert to the candid and honest opinion he then received, and determine, if ever he gets into another difficulty of the kind, to resort to that attorney, and abide by his advice. Thus may a man build up for himself a character far outweighing, even in pecuniary value, all such paltry particular losses; it is to such men that the best clients resort; they have the most important and interesting lawsuits, and enjoy by far the most lucrative practice.

A very important part of the advocate's duty is to moderate the passions of the party, and where the case is of a character to justify it, to encourage an amicable compromise of the controversy. It happens too often at the close of a protracted litigation that it is discovered, when too late, that the play has not been worth the candle, and that it would have been better, calculating everything, for the successful party never to have embarked in it—to have paid the claim, if defendant, or to have relinquished it, if he was plaintiff. Counsel can very soon discover whether such is likely to be the case, and it cannot be doubted what their plain duty is under such circumstances.

Besides this, the advocate is bound in honor, as well as duty, to disclose to the client at the time of the retainer, every circumstance of his own connection with the parties or prior relation to the controversy, which can or may influence his determination in the selection of him for the office. An attorney is bound to disclose to his client every adverse retainer, and even every prior retainer, which may affect the discretion of the latter. No man can be supposed to be indifferent to the knowledge of facts, which work directly on his interests, or bear on the freedom of his choice of counsel. When a client employs an attorney, he has a right to presume, if the latter be silent on the point, that he has no engagements which interfere, in any degree, with his exclusive devotion to the cause confided to him; that he has no interest which may betray his judgment or endanger his fidelity.*

It is in some measure the duty of counsel to be the keeper of the conscience of the client; not to suffer him, through the influence of his feelings or interest, to do or say anything wrong in itself, and of which he would himself afterwards repent. This guardianship may be carefully, and at the same time kindly exerted. One particular will be mentioned in which its exercise is frequently called for. The client will be often required, in the course of a cause, to make affidavits of various kinds. There is no part of his business with his client, in which a lawyer should be more cautious, or even punctilious, than this. He should be careful lest he incur the moral guilt of subornation of perjury, if not the legal offence. An attorney may have communications with his client in such a way, in instructing him as to

* Per Story, J., in Williams *v.* Read, 3 Mason, 418.

what the law requires him to state under oath or affirmation, in order to accomplish any particular object in view, as to offer an almost irresistible temptation and persuasion to stretch the conscience of the affiant up to the required point. Instead of drawing affidavits, and permitting them to be sworn to as a matter of course, as it is to be feared is too often the case, counsel should on all occasions take care to treat an oath with great solemnity, as a transaction to be very scrupulously watched, because involving great moral peril as well as liability to public disgrace and infamy. It lies especially in the way of the profession to give a high tone to public sentiment upon this all-important subject, the sacredness of an oath. It is always the wisest and best course, to have an interview with the client, and draw from him by questions, whether he knows the facts which you know he is required to state, so that you may judge whether, as a conscientious man, he ought to make such affidavit.

Another particular may be adverted to: the attempt to cover property from the just demands of creditors. It is to be feared that gentlemen of the Bar sometimes shut their eyes and, under the influence of feelings of commiseration for an unfortunate client, feign not to see what is really very palpable to everybody else. Surely they ought never to sanction, directly or indirectly such shams, especially when the machinery of a judicial sale is introduced more securely to accomplish the object. A purchase is made in the name of a friend for the debtor's benefit and with the debtor's money, though it may be hard to make that appear by legal evidence. When advice is asked, as it sometimes is, how such a thing may be safely and legally done, the idea held prominently before the party by his counsel should be, that his estate is the property of his creditors, and that nothing but their consent will justify an appropriation of any part of it to his benefit.

Lawyers too may very materially assist in giving a high tone to public sentiment in the matter of stay and exemption laws. It is not every case in which a man has a legal that he has a moral right to claim the benefit of such laws. When a debtor with ample means to pay only wants to harass and worry his creditor, who has resorted to legal process and obtained a judgment, by keeping him out of his money, as it is often expressed, as long as he can; or where he wishes to take advantage of hard times to make more than legal interest, or with concealed means unknown to the execution plaintiff, claims the exemption: these are cases which counsel ought to hold up in their proper light to those whom they advise, and wash their hands of the responsibility of them. According to the Jewish law, the cloak or outer garment, which was generally used by the poorer classes as a covering during sleep, could not be retained by the creditor to whom it had been given in pledge, and of course was exempt by law from seizure for debt; and our blessed Saviour, in his sermon on the mount, has been supposed to refer to this exemption law, when he said: "And if any man will sue thee at the law and take away thy coat, let him have thy cloak also;" that is, confine not yourself in your transactions with your fellowmen to giving them simply the strict measure of their legal rights: give them all that is honestly theirs as far as you have ability, whether the law affords them a remedy or not. There have been some noble instances of bankrupts who, upon subsequently retrieving their fortunes, have fully discharged all their old debts, principal and interest, though released or barred by the Statute of Limitations; but such instances would be more common if the spirit of the high and pure morality, which breathes through the sermon on the mount, prevailed more extensively.

An important clause in the official oath is "to delay no man's cause for lucre or malice." It refers, no doubt, primarily, to the cause intrusted to the attorney, and prohibits him from resorting to such means for the purpose of procuring more fees, or of indulging any feeling he may have against his client personally. Such conduct would be a clear case of a violation of the oath. But it is a question, also, whether the case generally, in which he is retained, is not comprehended.* How far, then, can he safely go in delaying the cause for the benefit of, and in pursuance of the instructions of his client? A man comes to him and says: "I have no defence to this claim; it is just and due, but I have not the means to pay it; I want all the time you can get for me." The best plan in such instances, is, no doubt, at once

* In enumerating the things to which every pleader of others' causes ought to have a regard, the Mirror of Justices says, "That he put no false dilatories into court, nor false witnesses, nor move or offer any false corruptive deceits, leasings, or false lies, nor consent to any such, but truly maintain his client's cause, so that it fail not by any negligence or default in him, nor by any threatening, hurt, or villany, disturb the judge, plaintiff, serjeant, or any other in court, whereby he hinder the right or the hearing of the cause." Chap. 2, s. 5. This is indeed in the very words of the serjeant's oath, and Lord Coke remarks that it consists of four parts: "1. That he shall well and truly serve the king's people, as one of the serjeants at law. 2. That he shall truly counsel them that he shall be retained with, after his cunning. 3. That he shall not defer, wait, or delay their causes willingly for covetousness of money, or other thing that may tend to his profit. 4. That he shall give due attendance accordingly." 2 Inst. 214.

frankly to address his opponent, and he will generally be willing to grant all the delay which he knows, in the ordinary course can be gained, and perhaps more, as a consideration for his own time and trouble saved. If, however, that be impracticable, it would seem that the suitor has a right to all the delay, which is incident to the ordinary course of justice. The counsel may take all means for this purpose, which do not involve artifice or falsehood in himself or the party. The formal pleas put in are not to be considered as false in this aspect, except such as are required to be sustained by oath. In an ejectment, for example, an appearance need not be entered until the second term, the legislature having seen fit to give that much respite to the unjust possessor of real estate. But to stand by and see a client swear off a case on account of the absence of a material witness, when he knows that no witness can be material; or further to make affidavit that his appeal or writ of error is not intended for delay, when he knows that it is intended for nothing else, no high-minded man will be privy or consent to such actions, much less have any active participation in them.

Subject, however, to the qualifications which have been stated, when a cause is undertaken, the great duty which the counsel owes to his client, is an immovable fidelity. Every consideration should induce an honest and honorable man to regard himself, as far as the cause is concerned, as completely identified with his client. The criminal and disgraceful offence of taking fees of two adversaries, of allowing himself to be approached corruptly, whether directly or indirectly, with a view to conciliation, ought, like parricide in the Athenian law, to be passed over in silence in a code of professional ethics.* All considerations of self should be sunk by the lawyer in his duty to the cause. The adversary may be a man of station, wealth, and influence; his good will may be highly valuable to him; his enmity may do him great injury. He should not per-

* A pleader is suspendable when he is attainted to have received fees of two adversaries, in one cause. Mirror of Justices, chap. 2, sect. 5.

mit such thoughts to arise in his mind. He should do his duty manfully, without fear, favor, or affection.

At the same time, let it be observed, that no man ought to allow himself to be hired to abuse the opposite party. It is not a desirable professional reputation to live and die with, that of a rough tongue, which makes a man to be sought out, and retained to gratify the malevolent feelings of a suitor in hearing the other side well lashed and vilified. An opponent should always be treated with civility and courtesy, and if it be necessary to say severe things of him or his witnesses, let it be done in the language, and with the bearing, of a gentleman. There is no point in which it becomes an advocate to be more cautious, than in his treatment of the witnesses. In general, fierce assaults upon them, unnecessary trifling with their feelings, rough and uncivil behavior towards them in cross-examination, whilst it may sometimes exasperate them to such a pitch, that they will perjure themselves in the drunkenness of their passion, still, most generally tells badly on the jury. They are apt to sympathize with a witness under such circumstances.* It is as well unwise as unprofessional, in counsel, to accuse a witness of having forsworn himself, unless some good ground, other than the mere instruction of the client, is present in the evidence to justify it. He may sift most searchingly, and yet with a manner and courtesy which affords no ground for irritation, either in witness or opponent; and in such case, if his questions produce irrita-

* "It is impossible to state a case, in which a witness should be treated roughly. If you attempt it, every one feels offended, in the person of the witness. You make your work more difficult; the witness shuts himself up, considers you as his enemy, and stands upon his defence: whereas, an open countenance, and an easy insinuating address, unlocks his breast, and disarms him of his caution, if he has any." Deinology, 228. This admirable little work, which has been attributed to the pen of Lord Erskine, cannot be too highly recommended to the student of law. The postscript, which suggests considerations on the *viva voce* examination of witnesses, is particularly worthy a very attentive perusal.

tion, it is a circumstance which will weigh in his favor.

The practitioner owes to his client, with unshaken fidelity, the exertion of all the industry and application of which he is capable to become perfect master of the questions at issue, to look at them in all their bearings, to place himself in the opposite interest, and to consider and be prepared as far as possible, for all that may be said or done on the contrary part. The duty of full and constant preparation, is too evident to require much elaboration. It is better, whenever it is possible to do so, to make this examination immediately upon the retainer, and not to postpone it to later stages in the proceedings. The opportunity is often lost, of ascertaining facts, and securing evidence, from putting off till too late, the business of understanding thoroughly all that it will be necessary to adduce on the trial. In this way, a lawyer will attain what is very important, that his client may be always prepared, as well as himself, have his attention alive to his case, know what witnesses are important, and keep a watch upon them, so that their testimony may not be lost, and upon the movements of his adversary, lest he should at any time be taken by surprise. It would be an excellent rule for him, at short stated periods, to make an examination of the record of every case which he has under his charge. It always operates disadvantageously to an attorney in the eyes of those who employ him, as well as the public, when he fails in consequence of some neglect or oversight. Frequent applications to the court, to relieve him from the consequences of his inattention, tell badly on his character and business. He may be able to make very plausible excuses; but the public take notice, that some men with large business never have occasion to make such excuses, and that other men with less, are constantly making them. Every instance of the kind helps to make up such a character. A young man should be particularly cautious, and dread such occurrences as highly injurious to his prospects. If he escapes the notice and animadversion of his constituent, and the legal consequences of his neglect, by the intervention of the court, or the indulgence of his opponent, the members of the Bar are lynx-eyed in observing such things.

It may appear like digressing from our subject, to speak of such qualities as attention, accuracy, and punctuality, but like the minor morals of common life, they are little rills which at times unite and form great rivers. A life of dishonor and obscurity, if not ignominy, has often taken its rise from the fountain of a little habit of inattention and procrastination. System is everything. It can accomplish wonders. By this alone, as by a magic talisman, may time be so economized that business can be attended to and opportunities saved for study, general reading, exercise, recreation, and society. "A man that is young in years," says Lord Bacon, "may be old in hours, if he has lost no time." Hurry and confusion result from the want of system; and the mind can never be clear when a man's papers and business are in disorder. It is recorded of the pensionary De Witt, of the United Provinces, who fell a victim to the fury of the populace in the year 1672, that he did the whole business of the republic, and yet had time left for relaxation and study in the evenings. When he was asked how he could possibly bring this to pass, his answer was, that "nothing was so easy; for that it was only doing one thing at a time, and never putting off anything till to-morrow that could be done to-day." "This steady and undissipated attention to one object," remarks Lord Chesterfield, in relating this anecdote, "is a sure mark of a superior genius." It is of the highest importance, also, that a lawyer should in early professional life, cultivate the habit of accuracy. It is a great advantage over opposing counsel,—a great recommendation in the eyes of intelligent mercantile and business men. A professional note to a merchant carelessly written will often of itself produce an unfavorable impression on his mind; and that impression he may communicate to many others. The importance of a good handwriting cannot be overrated. A plain legible hand every man can write who chooses to take the pains. A good handwriting is a passport to the favor of clients, and to the good graces of judges, when papers come to be submitted to them. It would be a good rule for a young lawyer, though at first perhaps irksome and inconvenient, never to suffer a letter or paper to pass from his hands with an erasure or interlineation. The time and trouble it may cost at the outset will be repaid in the end by the habit he will thereby acquire of transacting his business with care, neatness, and accuracy.

He cannot be faithful to his clients unless he continues to be a hard student of the learning of his profession. Not merely that he should thoroughly investigate the law applicable to every case which may be intrusted to him; though that, besides its paramount necessity to enable him to meet the responsibility he has assumed to that particular client, will be the subsidiary means of important progress in his professional acquisitions. "Let any person," says Mr. Preston, "study one or two heads of the law fully and minutely, and he will have laid the foundation or acquired the aptitude for comprehending other heads of the law."* But, besides this, he should pursue the systematic study of his profession upon some well-matured plan. When admitted to the Bar, a young man has but just begun, not finished, his legal education. If he have mastered some of the most general elementary principles, and has acquired a taste for the study, it is as much as can be expected from his clerkship. There are few young men who come to the Bar, who cannot find ample time in the first five or seven years of their novitiate, to devote to a complete acquisition of the science they profess, if they truly feel the need of it, and resolve to attain it. The danger is great that from a faulty preparation,—from not being made to see and appreciate the depth, extent, and variety of the knowledge they are to seek, they will mistake the smattering they have acquired for profound attainments. The anxiety of the young lawyer is a natural one at once to get business—as much business as

* Preston on Estates, 2.

he can. Throwing aside his books, he resorts to the many means at hand of gaining notoriety and attracting public attention, with a view of bringing clients to his office. Such an one in time never fails to learn much by his mistakes, but at a sad expense of character, feeling, and conscience. He at last finds that in law, as in every branch of knowledge, "a little learning is a dangerous thing;" that what he does not know falsifies often in its actual application that which he supposed he certainly did know; and after the most valuable portion of his life has been frittered away upon objects unworthy of his ambition, he is too apt to conclude that it is now too late to redeem his time; he finds that he has lost all relish for systematic study, and when he is driven to the investigation of particular questions, is confounded and embarrassed—unable to thread his way through the mazes of authorities, to reconcile apparently conflicting cases, or deduce any satisfactory conclusion from them—in short, he has no greater aptitude, accuracy, and discrimination than when he set out in the beginning of his studies. No better advice can be given to a young practitioner, than to confine himself generally to his office and books, even if this should require self-denial and privation, to map out for himself a course of regular studies, more or less extended, according to circumstances, to aim at mastering the works of the great luminaries of the science, Coke, Fearne, Preston, Powell, Sugden, and others, not forgetting the maxim, *melius est petere fontes quam sectari rivulos,* and to investigate for himself the most important and interesting questions, by an examination and research of the original authorities. "He that reacheth deepest seeth the amiable and admirable secrets of the law,"* and thus may the student "proceed in his reading with alacrity, and set upon and know how to work into with delight these rough mines of hidden treasure."†

It may be allowed here to commend to most serious consideration, the remarks of one

* Co. Litt. 71 *a.*

† Ibid. 6 *a.*

of the most eminent of the profession—Horace Binney—a gentleman of our own Bar, whose example enforces and illustrates their value: "There are two very different methods of acquiring a knowledge of the laws of England, and by each of them, men have succeeded in public estimation to an almost equal extent. One of them, which may be called the old way, is a methodical study of the general system of law, and of its grounds and reasons, beginning with the fundamental law of estates and tenures, and pursuing the derivative branches in logical succession, and the collateral subjects in due order; by which the student acquires a knowledge of principles that rule in all departments of the science, and learns to feel as much as to know what is in harmony with the system and what not. The other is, to get an outline of the system, by the aid of commentaries, and to fill it up by the desultory reading of treatises and reports, according to the bent of the student, without much shape or certainty in the knowledge so acquired, until it is given by investigation in the course of practice. A good deal of law may be put together by a facile or flexible man, in the second of these modes, and the public are often satisfied; but the profession itself knows the first, by its fruits, to be the most effectual way of making a great lawyer."*

* Art. Edward Tilghman, in the Encyclopædia Americâna, vol. xiv; The Leaders of the Old Bar of Philadelphia, 50. Let me recommend to the attention of the student a curious and interesting work, entitled "An introduction to the science of the law, showing the advantages of a legal education, grounded on the learning of Lord Coke's Commentaries, upon Littleton's Tenures, &c., by Frederick Ritso, Esq." There are few works of celebrity, in regard to which such opposite opinions have been maintained as the Commentaries of Sir William Blackstone. While some have expressed the most enthusiastic admiration, there have been others, like Mr. Austin, Professor of General Jurisprudence, in the University of London (Outlines of Lectures, 63), who have dealt in language of unsparing condemnation and contempt. Mr. Ritso thinks that "the error was in adopting them as an institute for the instruction and education of professional students, which was evidently no part of Blackstone's plan, nor within the scope of his engagement." In this point of view, he objects, that "he represents everything rather for effect, than with a view to demonstrate. Like the gnomon upon

Such a course of study as is here recommended, is not the work of a day or a year.

the sun-dial, he takes no account of any hours, but the serene:

> Et quæ,
> Desperat tractata nitescere posse, relinquit.

In a professional point of view, this solicitude rather to captivate the imagination of the student, than to exercise and discipline the understanding, is equally unprofitable and inconvenient. It puts him off with ornamental illustration, instead of solid argument, and leads to a sort of half information, which is often much worse than no information at all upon the subject." There is some force in these remarks; yet, too many great lawyers have begun their studies with Blackstone, to leave any doubt that it is a proper first book. It paves the way for more repulsive, though more recondite and valuable works. I very much fear, indeed, that a disposition has existed of late years to repudiate Coke upon Littleton entirely. Chancellor Kent has shown his leaning in that direction (Comm. vol. i, 506, 512). I subscribe fully, however, to Mr. Butler's opinion: "He is the best lawyer, and will succeed best in his profession, who best understands Coke upon Littleton." It ought not, perhaps, to be placed in the hands of the student until he has made some progress in his reading of other works: but sooner or later, he should aim to master

In the meantime let business seek the young attorney; and though it may come in slowly, and at intervals, and promise in its character neither fame nor profit, still, if he bears in mind that it is an important part of his training, that he should understand the business he does thoroughly, that he should especially cultivate, in transacting it, habits of neatness, accuracy, punctuality, and despatch, candor towards his client, and strict honor towards his adversary, it may be safely prophesied that his business will grow as fast as it is good for him that it should grow; while he gradually becomes able to sustain the largest practice, without being bewildered and overwhelmed.

it. Lord Coke was, himself, deeply imbued with the love of his profession, and he is able to transfuse his own spirit into his readers. His method may be objectionable in some respects; but I cannot help thinking that the life of his work is gone when it is hacked to pieces, and then attempted to be fitted together again upon another man's skeleton. I have ventured to add in the Appendix (No. II), a sketch of such a course of reading, of not very extensive compass, as may with advantage be pursued by every young man after his admission to the Bar.

Let him be careful, however, not to settle down into a mere lawyer. To reach the highest walks of the profession, something more is needed. Let polite literature be cultivated in hours of relaxation. Let him lose not his acquaintance with the models of ancient taste and eloquence. He should study languages, as well from their practical utility in a country so full of foreigners, as from the mental discipline, and the rich stores they furnish. He should cultivate a pleasing style, and an easy and graceful address. It may be true, that in a "court of justice, the veriest dolt that ever stammered a sentence, would be more attended to, with a case in point, than Cicero with all his eloquence, unsupported by authorities,"* yet even an argument on a dry point of law, produces a better impression, secures a more attentive auditor in the judge, when it is constructed and put together with attention to the rules of the rhetorical art; when it is delivered, not stammeringly, but fluently; when facts and

* Maddock's Chancery. Preface.

principles, drawn from other fields of knowledge, are invoked to support and adorn it; when voice, and gesture, and animation, give it all that attraction which earnestness always and alone imparts. There is great danger that law reading, pursued to the exclusion of everything else, will cramp and dwarf the mind, shackle it by the technicalities with which it has become so familiar, and disable it from taking enlarged and comprehensive views even of topics falling within its compass as well as of those lying beyond its legitimate domain. An amusing instance of this is said to have occurred in the debate in the House of Commons, on the great question as to the right of the Parliament of Great Britain to tax the Colonies. At the close of the discussion, in which Fox and Burke, as well as others, had distinguished themselves, a learned lawyer arose and said that the real point on which the whole matter turned, had been unaccountably overlooked. In the midst of deep silence and anxious expectation from all quarters of the House, he proceeded to show that the lands of the Colonies had been originally granted by the Crown, and were held *ut de honore*, as of the Manor of Greenwich, in the county of Kent; and thence he concluded that as the Manor of Greenwich was represented in Parliament, so the lands of the North American Colonies (by tenure, a part of the Manor) were represented by the knights of the shire for Kent.*

Let me remark, too, before hastening to another topic more immediately connected with the duties of active professional life, that the cultivation of a taste for polite literature has other importance besides its value as a prepa-

* Bowyer's Readings on the Canon Law, p. 44. Lord Campbell says that the person here mentioned was George Hardinge—a Welsh judge and nephew of Lord Camden. 5 Lives of the Chancellors, 20, 281. According to Lord Mahon, it was on the 15th of March, 1782, in the debate on a motion of Sir John Rouse, of want of confidence in the ministry after the surrender of Lord Cornwallis. He ascribes the remark to Sir James Marriott, but says that, although he was the assertor of this singular argument, the honor of its original invention seems rather to belong to Mr. Hardinge. 5 Mahon's Hist. 139.

ration and qualification for practice and forensic contests. Nothing is so well adapted to fill up the interstices of business with rational enjoyment, to make even a solitary life agreeable, and to smooth pleasantly and honorably the downward path of age. The mental vigor of one who is fond of reading, other things being equal, becomes impaired at a much later period of life. The lover of books has faithful companions and friends, who will never forsake him under the most adverse circumstances. "As soon as I found," said Sir Samuel Romilly, "that I was to be a busy lawyer for life, I strenuously resolved to keep up my habit of non-professional reading; for I had witnessed so much misery in the last years of many great lawyers, whom I had known, from their loss of all taste for books, that I regarded their fate as my warning." Mr. Gibbon was wont to say that he would not exchange his love of reading for the wealth of the Indies. It is indeed a fortune, of which the world's reverses can never deprive us. It fortifies the soul against the calamities of life. It moderates, if it is not strong enough to govern and control the passions. It favors not the association of the cup, the dice-box, or the debauch. The atmosphere of a library is uncongenial with them. It clings to home, nourishes the domestic affections, and the hopes and consolations of religion.

Another very delicate and often embarrassing question in the relation of attorney and client is in regard to the subject of compensation for professional services.

In all countries advanced in civilization, and whose laws and manners have attained any degree of refinement, there has arisen an order of advocates devoted to prosecuting or defending the lawsuits of others. Before the tribunals of Athens, although the party pleaded his own cause, it was usual to have the oration prepared by one of an order of men devoted to this business, and to compensate him liberally for his skill and learning. Many of the orations of Isocrates, which have been handed down to us, are but private pleadings of this character. He is said to have received one fee of twenty talents, about eighteen thousand dollars of our money, for a speech that he wrote for Nicocles, king of Cyprus. Still, from all that appears, the compensation thus received was honorary or gratuitous merely. Among the early institutions of Rome, the relation of patron and client, which existed between the patrician and plebeian, bound the former to render the latter assistance and protection in his lawsuits, with no other return than the general duty, which the client owed to his patron. As every patrician could not be a sufficiently profound lawyer to resolve all difficulties, which might arise in the progress of a complex system of government and laws, though he still might accomplish himself in the art of eloquence, there arose soon a new order of men, the jurisconsults. They also received no compensation. On the public days of market, or assembly, the masters of the art were seen walking in the forum, ready to impart the needful advice to the meanest of their fellow-citizens, from whose votes on a future occasion, they might solicit a grateful return. As their years and honors increased, they seated themselves at home, on a chair or throne, to expect with patient gravity the visits of their clients, who at the dawn of day, from the town and country, began to thunder at their doors.* Often, indeed, the patron was able in his own person to exercise the office both of advocate and counsellor. It was only in the more glorious, because the more virtuous, period of the republic, that the relation was sustained upon so honorable a foundation. In the progress of society, the business of advocating causes became a distinct profession; and then it was usual to pay a fee in advance, which was called a gratuity or present. As this was a mere honorary recompense, the client was under no legal obligation to pay it. But the result necessarily was, that if the usual present was not given, the advocate did not consider himself bound in honor to undertake the advocation of the cause before the courts. Afterwards, Marcus Cincius Alimentus, the

* Gibbon's Decline and Fall of the Roman Empire, c. xliv.

tribune of the people, procured the passage of the law known as the *Cincian* law, prohibiting the patron or advocate from receiving any money or other present for any cause; and annulling all gratuities or presents made by the client to the patron or advocate. But as no penalty was prescribed for the breach of the law, it of course became a dead letter. The Emperor Augustus afterwards re-enacted the Cincian law, and prescribed penalties for its breach. But towards the end of his reign, the advocates were again authorized to receive fees or presents from their clients. The Emperor Tiberius also permitted them to receive such forced gratuities. This led to the abuse referred to by Tacitus, and induced the Senate to insist upon the enforcement of the re-enactment of the Cincian law, or rather a law limiting the amount of the fees of advocates.* Nero re-

* Continuus inde et sævus accusandis reis Sicilius, multique audaciæ ejus æmuli. Nam cuncta legum et magistratuum munia in se trahens Princeps, materiam prædandi patefecerat. Nec quidquam publicæ mercis tam venale fuit, quam advocatorum perfidia: adeo ut Samius insignis

voked the law of Claudian, which was subsequently re-enacted by the Emperor Trajan, with the additional restriction that the advocate should not be permitted to receive his fee or gratuity, until the cause was decided. The younger Pliny mentions a law, which authorized the advocate, after the pleadings in the cause had been made and the judgment had been given, to receive the fee, which might be voluntarily offered by the client, either in money or a promise to pay. Erskine, in his Institutes of the Law of Scotland, understands the law in the Digest *De Extraordinariis Cognitionibus* as authorizing a suit for the fee of a physician or advocate without a previous agreement for a specific sum.*

eques Romanus, quadringentis nummorum millibus, Sicilio datis, et cognita prevaricatione, ferro in domo ejus incubuerit. Igitur incipiente C. Silio consule designato, cujus de potentia et exitio in tempore memorabo, consurgunt patres, legemque Cinciam flagitant, qua cavetur antiquitus ne quis ob causam orandam pecuniam donumve accipiat. Tacit. Annal. l. 11, c. 5.

* Chancellor Walworth, in Adams *v.* Stevens, 26 Wen-

The consequences may be best told in the impressive language of the historian of the Decline and Fall of the Empire: "The noble art, which had once been preserved as the sacred inheritance of the patricians, was fallen into the hands of freedmen and plebeians, who, with cunning rather than with skill, exercised a sordid and pernicious trade. Some of them procured admittance into families for the purpose of fomenting differences, of encouraging suits, and of preparing a harvest of gain for themselves or their brethren. Others, recluse in their chambers, maintained the dignity of legal professors, by furnishing a rich client with subtleties to confound the plainest truth, and

dell, 21. While expressing, as will be seen presently, the opinion that authority as well as sound policy would have led me to a different conclusion from that at which Chancellor Walworth arrived, it is proper to acknowledge that I have drawn largely upon his learned judgment in this case, and at the same time to express the high admiration I entertain for the ability with which the last of the New York Chancellors illustrated the chair where such truly great men had sat before him.

with arguments to color the most unjustifiable pretensions. The splendid and popular class was composed of the advocates, who filled the Forum with the sound of their turgid and loquacious rhetoric. Careless of fame and of justice, they are described for the most part, as ignorant and rapacious guides, who conducted their clients through a maze of expense, of delay, and of disappointment; from whence, after a tedious series of years, they were at length dismissed when their patience and fortune were almost exhausted."* Is not this probably the history of the decline of the profession in all countries from an honorable office to a money-making trade?

It is the established law of England, that a counsellor or barrister cannot maintain a suit for his fees.† There is in that country a class

* Gibbon's Decline and Fall, c. xvii.

† 3 Blackst. Com. 28; Davis Pref. 22; 1 Chanc. Rep. 38; Davis, 23; Hodgson *v.* Scarlett, 1 B. & Ald. 232; Finch. L. 188; and see Butler's note to 1 Co. Litt. 295 a. So it is with the advocates in the civil law. Vost ad Pand. tit. de Postul. Numb. 6, 7, 8; Gravina de Oster. lib. 1, s.

of mere attorneys, who attend to legal business out of court, who bring suits and conduct them up to issue; but who are not allowed to speak in court. This latter privilege is confined to serjeants and barristers. Attorneys are regulated by statute, and are subject to many restrictions; having a rate of fees, settled either by statute or established usage; and required

42, 43, 44. Boucher D'Asyis, Hist. Abrégé de L'Order des Avocats, c. iv. See also the commencement of the Dialogue des Avocats du Parl. de Paris, by Loisil, which contains curious particulars throughout respecting the ancient French Bar. An amusing anecdote is related of Pasquier, the famous French advocate. In 1583, while he was attending the assizes (*les grands jours*) at Troyes, he sat for his portrait, and after the painter had finished the likeness, which Pasquier had not yet examined, he asked him to represent him with a book in his hand. The painter said that it was too late, as the picture was completed without hands. Upon this the witty lawyer immediately wrote the following lines as a motto for the portrait:

> Nulla hic Pascasio manus est: Lex Cincia quippe
> Causidicos nulla sanxit habere manus.

Forsyth's Hortensius, 424.

to be fixed by the taxation of an officer of the court before a suit can be brought for them. Barristers are admitted only under the regulations established by the various inns of court; and the serjeants, who long had the monopoly of the Bar of the Common Pleas, are appointed by patent from the king. A barrister cannot be an attorney.*

In this country, there is in general no distinction between attorneys and counsellors. The same persons fulfil the duties of both. Hence no difference is made between their right to recover compensation for services in the one capacity or the other.† In Pennsylvania, it was held at one time that an attorney

* The reader will find in the Appendix, No. III, an account of the different orders of the English Bar.

† In some States, the professions of attorney and counsellor at law are not distinct; the same person conducts the cause in all its stages; and it has not been considered that his authority ceases when judgment is obtained. The attorney is in some degree the agent as well as the attorney of the party. Huston, J., in Lynch *v.* The Commonwealth, 16 Serg. & Rawle, 368.

could not recover, without an express promise, anything beyond the trifling and totally inadequate sum provided in the fee-bill. That pure and eminent jurist Chief Justice Tilghman thought that the policy of refusing a legal remedy for anything beyond that had not been adopted without great consideration.* He stands not alone in the opinion that it has been neither for the honor nor profit of the Bar to depart from the ancient rule.† It has been departed from in this State, and the early decision overruled, however; and it must be frankly admitted, that the current of decisions in our sister States is in the same way.‡

* Mooney *v.* Lloyd, 5 Serg. & Rawle, 416.

† Hornblower, C. J., in Seeley et al. *v.* Crane, 3 Green, N. J. 35. "I shall be sorry to see the honorary character of the fees of barristers and physicians done away with. Though it seems to be a shadowy distinction, yet I believe it to be beneficial in effect. It contributes to preserve the idea of profession, of a class which belongs to the public, in the employment and remuneration of which no law interferes, but the citizen acts as he likes, '*foro conscientiæ.*'" Coleridge's Table Talk, vol. 2.

‡ Gray *v.* Brackenridge, 2 Penna. Rep. 181; Foster *v.*

It is supposed that the ancient rule was artificial in its structure, and practically unjust,—that it is wholly inconsistent with our ideas of equality to suppose that the business or profession, by which any one earns the daily bread of himself or of his family, is so much more honorable than the business of other members of the community as to prevent him from receiving a fair compensation for his services on that account.* It has been pronounced ridicu-

Jack, 4 Watts, 33. In New Jersey, an advocate's fees are not recoverable at law. Shaver *v.* Norris, Penning. 63; Seeley *v.* Crane, 3 Green, 35; Van Alter *v.* McKinney's Exrs. 1 Harrison, 236. That the general current of decisions is in the opposite direction, will be seen by consulting Stevens *v.* Adams, 23 Wendell, 57; S. C. 26 Wendell, 451; Newman *v.* Washington, Martin & Yerger, 79; Stevens *v.* Monges, 1 Harrington, 127; Bayard *v.* McLane, 3 Harrington, 217; Duncan *v.* Beisthaupt, 1 McCord, 149; Downing *v.* Major, 2 Dana, 228; Christy *v.* Douglas, Wright's Ch. Rep. 485; Webb *v.* Hepp, 14 Missouri, 354; Vilas *v.* Downer, 21 Vermont, 419; Lecatt *v.* Sallee, 3 Porter, 115; Easton *v.* Smith, 1 E. D. Smith, 318.

* Chancellor Walworth, in Adams *v.* Stevens, 26 Wendell, 451; Foster *v.* Jack, 4 Watts, 337.

lous to attempt to perpetuate a monstrous legal fiction, by which the hard-working lawyers of our day, toiling till midnight in their offices, are to be regarded in the eye of the law in the light of the patrician jurisconsults of ancient Rome, when

> —— dulce diu fuit et solemne, reclusa
> Mane domo vigilare, clienti promere jura,—

and who at daybreak received the early visits of their humble and dependent clients, and pronounced with mysterious brevity the oracles of the law.*

These are arguments which are more plausible than sound: they are imposing, but not solid. The question really is, what is best for the people at large,—what will be most likely to secure them a high-minded, honorable Bar? It is all-important that the profession should have and deserve that character. A horde of pettifogging, barratrous, custom-seeking,

* Senator Verplanck, in Adams *v.* Stevens, 26 Wendell, 451.

money-making lawyers, is one of the greatest curses with which any state or community can be visited. What more likely to bring about such a result than a decision, which strips the Bar of its character as a learned profession, on the principle avowed by one court, that it is now a calling as much as any mechanical art,—or by another, in effect, that the order of things is in the present condition of society reversed, and clients are really the *patrons* of their attorneys? A more plausible reason is that the client is safer from the oppression of extortionate counsel, by putting both upon the equal footing of legal right and obligation. It would appear, however, better that the parties should make an express agreement before or at the time of retainer, or that the amount should be left to the justice of the counsel, and the honor and liberality of the client subsequently. Every judge, who has ever tried a case between attorney and client, has felt the delicacy and difficulty of saying what is the measure of just compensation. It is to be graduated, according to a high legal authority, with a proper reference to the nature of the business performed by the counsel for the client, and his standing in his profession for learning and skill; whereby the value of his services is enhanced to his client.* Is then the standing and character of the counsel in his profession for learning and skill to be a question of fact to be determined by the jury in every case in which a lawyer sues his client? How determined, if necessary to the decision of the question? Not surely by the crude opinions of the jurors; but by testimony of members of the same profession on the subject. This never is done; it would be a very difficult as well as delicate question for a lawyer to pronounce upon the standing of a professional brother. The most that can be done is to call gentlemen to say what they would have considered reasonable for such services, had

* Vilas *v.* Downer, 21 Vermont, 419. Responsibility in a confidential employment is a legitimate subject of compensation, and in proportion to the magnitude of the interests committed to the agent. Kentucky Bank *v.* Combs, 7 Barr, 543.

they been performed by themselves. Some may testify up to a very high point, from an excusable, though foolish vanity; others to a very low one, from the despicable desire of attracting custom to a cheap shop.* No one can ever have seen such a cause tried without feeling, that the Bar had received by it an impulse downwards in the eyes of bystanders and the community. The case is thrown into the jury-box, to be decided at haphazard, according as the twelve men may chance to think or feel. He, who narrowly watches such controversies, cannot fail to see that the right of a counsel to enforce his claim for legal compensation is far from being calculated to protect the client from oppression and extortion.

It is not worth while, however, to quarrel with the decision. Let us inquire rather what should be the course of counsel, without regard to it. He certainly owes it to his profession,

* That evidence of usage is admissible to show what is the rule of compensation for similar services to those sued for, see Vilas *v.* Downer, 21 Vermont, 424; Badfish *v.* Fox, 23 Maine, 94.

as well as himself, that when the client has the ability, his services should be recompensed; and that according to a liberal standard.* There are many cases, in which it will be his duty, perhaps more properly his privilege, to work for nothing. It is to be hoped, that the time will never come, at this or any other Bar in this country, when a poor man with an honest cause, though without a fee, cannot obtain the services of honorable counsel, in the prosecution or defence of his rights. But it must be an extraordinary—a very peculiar case—that will justify an attorney in resorting to legal proceedings, to enforce the payment of fees. It is better that he should be a loser, than have a public contest upon the subject with a client. The enlightened Bar of Paris, have justly considered the character of their order involved in such proceedings; and al-

* Concerning the pleader's salary, says the Mirror, chap. 2, sec. 5, "four things are to be regarded: 1. The greatness of the cause. 2. The pains of the serjeant. 3. His worth, as his learning, eloquence, and gift. 4. The usage of the court."

though by the law of France, an advocate may recover for his fees by suit, yet they regard it as dishonorable, and those who should attempt to do it, would be immediately stricken from the roll of attorneys.*

* Les lois et les docteurs, les anciennes ordonnances et plusieurs anciens arrêts donnent aux avocats une action pour le paiement de leurs honoraires : mais, suivant la dernière jurisprudence du Parlement de Paris et la discipline actuelle du barreau, ou ne souffre point qu'un avocat intente une telle action. 1 Dupin, Profession d'Avocat, 110. Il est possible, que l'usage ne soit qu'un préjugé; mais ce préjugé a eu une salutaire influence sur la splendeur du barreau Francais. On ne prétend pas, en France, qu'un avocat n'a pas droit à un honoraire pour prix de ses travaux. Jamais on n'a refusé d'en allouer à ceux qui en ont réclamé. Dans plusieurs barreaux, ces réclamations sont même tolerées. Mais le barreau de Paris s'est montré plus sévère; et non seulement autrefois, mais encore aujourd'hui, tout avocat à la cour qui actionnerait un client en paiement d'honoraires serait rayé du tableau. Du reste, s'il est defendu d'exiger, il est permis de recevoir tout ce que le client veut bien assigner pour prix aux services de son avocat, en raison de ses peines et de l'importance des travaux. Ibid. 698.

Les honoraires dus par les parties aux avocats chargés du

Regard should be had to the general usage of the profession, especially as to the rates of commission to be charged for the collection of undefended claims. Except in this class of cases, agreements between counsel and client that the compensation of the former shall depend upon final success in the lawsuit—in other words contingent fees—however common such agreements may be, are of a very dangerous tendency, and to be declined in all ordinary cases. In making his charge, after the business committed to him has been completed, as an attorney may well take into consideration the general ability of his client to pay, so he may also consider the pecuniary benefit, which may have been derived from his services. For a poor man, who is unable to pay at all, there may be a general understanding that the attorney is to be liberally compensated in case

soin de leur défense, ne doivent pas être restreints à la taxe établie par le tarif. Cette taxe a pour objet seulement de fixer la somme due par la partie qui succombe, et non d'apprecier les soins de l'avocat, appreciation qui doit etre faite selon l'importance et la difficulté du travail. Ibid. 699.

of success. What is objected to, is an agreement to receive a certain part or proportion of the sum, or subject-matter, in the event of a recovery, and nothing otherwise.

It is unnecessary to inquire here whether such a contract is void as champertous, and contrary to public policy. None of the English statutes on the subject of champerty have been reported as in force here; but it was once a question whether it was not an offence at common law, independently altogether, of any statute enactment. Enlightened judges in several of our sister States have so considered it. "The purchase of a lawsuit," says Chancellor Kent, "by an attorney, is champerty in its most odious form; and it ought equally to be condemned on principles of public policy. It would lead to fraud, oppression, and corruption. As a sworn minister of the courts of justice, the attorney ought not to be permitted to avail himself of the knowledge he acquires in his professional character, to speculate in lawsuits. The precedent would tend to corrupt the profession, and produce lasting mischief to the community."* "This is not the time nor place," says Chief Justice Gibson, "to discuss the legality of contingent fees; though it be clear that if the British statutes of champerty were in force here, such fees would be prohibited by them. But a contract of the sort is certainly not to be encouraged by implication, from a questionable usage, nor established by less than a positive stipulation."† A contract to allow a compensation for services in procuring the passage of a private Act of Assembly, has been held to be unlawful and void, as against public policy.‡

* Arden *v.* Patterson, 5 Johns. Ch. Rep. 48.

† Foster *v.* Jack, 4 Watts, 338, 339.

‡ Clippinger *v.* Hepbaugh, 5 Watts. & Serg. 315; Marshall *v.* The Baltimore and Ohio Railroad Co., 16 Howard (S. C.) Rep. 336. That champerty is an offence at common law, and that contracts of that character, between client and counsel, are void on that ground, and as against public policy, will be found to have been maintained in Rust *v.* Larue, 4 Litt. 411; Caldwell's Administrators *v.* Shepherd's Heirs, 6 Monroe, 391; Thurston *v.* Percival, 1 Pick. 415; Arden *v.* Patterson, 5 Johns. Ch. Rep. 48; Bleakley's case, 5 Paige, 311; Wallis *v.* Loubert, 2 Denio,

"The practice," said Judge Rogers, in delivering the opinion of the court, "which has

607; Backus *v.* Byron, 4 Michigan, 535; Elliott *v.* McClelland, 17 Alabama, 206. The cases on the other side, are, Thallhimer *v.* Brinckerhoff, 3 Cowen, 643; Ramsay's Devisees *v.* Trent, 10 B. Monroe, 336; Bayard *v.* McLane, 3 Harrington, 216; Lytle *v.* State, 17 Arkansas, 608; Newkirk *v.* Cone, 18 Illinois, 449; Major *v.* Gibson, 1 Patton Jr. & Heath (Va.), 48; Wright *v.* Meek, 3 Iowa, 472. In New York, by the Revised Statutes, it was made an offence, punishable by fine or imprisonment, and removal from the Bar, for any attorney, counsellor, or solicitor, directly or indirectly to buy, or be in any manner interested in buying, or to advance or procure money to be advanced upon anything in action, with the intent, or for the purpose of bringing any suit thereon. 2 Revised Stat. 386. The Code of Procedure appears to have changed the law in this respect, and to enable parties to make such bargains as they please with their attorneys. Code of Procedure, s. 258; Satterlee *v.* Frazer, 2 Sandf. S. C. Rep. 142; Benedict *v.* Stuart, 23 Barb. 420; Ogden *v.* Des Arts, 4 Duer (N. Y.), 275; Sedgwick *v.* Stanton, 4 Kernan, 289. In Kentucky there appears to be a statute, which provides that any one not a party, receiving as compensation for services in prosecuting or defending a suit the whole or part of the subject-matter in suit, is guilty of champerty, and it has been held that this statute extends to attorneys. Davis *v.*

generally obtained in this State, to allow a contingent compensation for legal services, has been a subject of regret; nor am I aware of any direct decision by which the practice has received judicial sanction in our courts." The case of *Ex parte Plitt*,* however, recognizes fully the lawfulness of contingent fees, though in his opinion Judge Kane says: "It is not a practice to be generally commended, exposing honorable men not unfrequently to misapprehension and illiberal remark, and giving the apparent sanction of their example to conduct, which they would be among the foremost to reprehend. Such contracts may sometimes be necessary in a community such as that of Pennsylvania has been, and perhaps as it is yet; and when they have been made in abundant good faith—*uberrima fide*—without suppression or reserve of fact or exaggeration of apprehended difficulties, or under in-

Sharron, 15 B. Monroe, 64. In England, contingent fees are held to be clearly within the statutes of champerty and maintenance. Penrice *v.* Parker, Rep. Temp. Finch, 75.

* 2 Wallace, Jr. Rep. 452.

fluence of any sort or degree; and when the compensation bargained for is absolutely just and fair, so that the transaction is characterized throughout by 'all good fidelity to the client,' the court will hold such contracts to be valid. But it is unnecessary to say, that such contracts, as they can scarcely be excepted from the general rule, which denounces as suspicious the dealings of fiduciaries with those under their protection, must undergo the most exact and jealous scrutiny before they can expect the judicial ratification." Finally, the question of law may be considered as at rest in Pennsylvania by the decision of the Supreme Court in Patten *v.* Wilson,* which recognized an agreement between counsel and client to pay him out of the verdict as an equitable assignment, and gave effect to it as against an attaching creditor.

It is not, however, with the lawfulness, but with the policy and morality of the practice, that we are now dealing. Admitting its le-

* 10 Casey, 299.

gality, is it consistent with that high standard of moral excellence, which the members of this profession should ever propose to themselves?

Let us look at what would be the results of such a practice, if it became general. If these are bad, if its tendency is to corrupt and degrade the character of the profession, then, however confident any man may feel in his moral power to ward off its evil influences from his own character and conduct, he should be careful not to encourage and give countenance to it by his example.

It is one of that class of actions, which in particular instances may be indifferent; but their morality is to be tested by considering what would be the consequences of their general prevalence.

It is to be observed, then, that such a contract changes entirely the relation of counsel, to the cause. It reduces him from his high position of an officer of the court and a minister of justice, to that of a party litigating his own claim. Having now a deep personal interest in the event of the controversy, he will cease to consider himself subject to the ordinary rules of professional conduct. He is tempted to make success, at all hazards and by all means, the sole end of his exertions. He becomes blind to the merits of the case, and would find it difficult to persuade himself, no matter what state of facts might be developed in the progress of the proceedings, as to the true character of the transaction, that it was his duty to retire from it.

It places his client and himself in a new and dangerous relation. They are no longer attorney and client, but partners. He has now an interest, which gives him a right to speak as principal, not merely to advise as to the law, and abide by instructions. It is either unfair to him or unfair to the client. If he thinks the result doubtful, he throws all his time, learning, and skill away upon what, in his estimation, is an uncertain chance. He cannot work with the proper spirit in such a case. If he believes that the result will be success, he secures in this way a higher compensation than he is justly entitled to receive.

It is an undue encouragement to litigation. Men, who would not think of entering on a lawsuit, if they knew that they must compensate their lawyer whether they win or lose, are ready upon such a contingent agreement to try their chances with any kind of a claim. It makes the law more of a lottery than it is.

The worst consequence is yet to be told,—its effect upon professional character. It turns lawyers into higglers with their clients. Of course it is not meant that these are always its actual results; but they are its inevitable tendencies,—in many instances its practical working. To drive a favorable bargain with the suitor in the first place, the difficulties of the case are magnified and multiplied, and advantage taken of that very confidence, which led him to intrust his interests to the protection of the advocate.* The parties are necessarily not on an

* Paciscendi quidem ille piraticus mos, et imponentium periculis pretia, procul abominanda negotiatio, etiam a mediocriter improbis aberit: cum præsertim bonos homines bonasque causas tuenti non sit metuendus ingratus, qui si futurus, malo tamen ille peccet. Quinct. Lib. xii, c. 7.

equal footing in making such a bargain. A high sense of honor may prevent counsel from abusing his position and knowledge; but all have not such high and nice sense of honor. If our example goes towards making the practice of agreements for contingent fees general, we assist in placing such temptations in the way of our professional brethren of all degrees—the young, the inexperienced, and the unwary, as well as those whose age and experience have taught them that a lawyer's honor is his brightest jewel, and to be guarded from being sullied, even by the breath of suspicion, with the most sedulous care.

A gentleman of the largest experience and highest character for integrity and learning at the Philadelphia Bar, thus strongly confirms the views which have been here expressed on the subject of contingent fees: "And further," says Mr. Price in his concluding advice to students, at the close of his Essay on Limitation and Lien, "permit me to advise and earnestly to admonish you, for the preservation of professional honor and integrity, to avoid the temptation of bargaining for fees or shares of any estate or other claim, contingent upon a successful recovery. The practice directly leads to a disturbance of the peace of society and to an infidelity to the professional obligation promised to the court, in which is implied an absence of desire or effort of one in the ministry of the Temple of Justice, to obtain a success that is not just as well as lawful. It is true, as a just equivalent for many cases honorably advocated and incompetently paid by the poor, a compensation may and will be received, the more liberal because of the ability produced by success; but let it be the result of no bargain, exacted as a price before the service is rendered, but rather the grateful return for benefits already conferred. If rigid in your terms, in protection of the right of the profession to a just and honorable compensation, let it rather be in the amount of the required retainer, when it will have its proper influence in the discouragement of litigation."

A lawyer should avoid, as far as possible, all transactions of business with his clients, not only in regard to matters in suit in his hands, but in relation to other matters. He should avoid standing toward them, either in the relation of borrower or lender. A young practitioner should especially avoid borrowing of any one. Let him retrench, seek the humblest employment of drudgery rather than do it; but, if borrow he must, let it be of any one else than a client. All transactions of business between attorney and client are looked upon with eyes of suspicion and disfavor, in courts of justice.

It is a settled doctrine of equity, in England, that an attorney cannot, while the business is unfinished in which he had been employed, receive any gift from his client, or bind his client in any mode to make him greater compensation for his services than he would have a right to demand if no contract should be made during the relation. If an attorney accept a gift from one thus connected with him, it may be recovered in a court of chancery, by the donor or his creditors, should it be necessary for them to assert a right to it to satisfy their demands.

When the relation of solicitor and client exists, and a security is taken by the solicitor from his client, the presumption is that the transaction is unfair; and the onus of proving its fairness is upon the solicitor.* A man ought to be very careful of placing himself in a position to have any of his transactions regarded in that light. If it should ever come to be canvassed in court, the bandying of the

* Evans *v.* Ellis, 5 Denio, 640; Newman *v.* Payne, 2 Ves. 199; Walmsley *v.* Booth, 3 Atk. 25; Montesquieu *v.* Sandys, 18 Ves. 313. The doctrine has been fully followed in this country; Stockton *v.* Ford, 11 How. U. S. 247; Starr *v.* Vanderheyden, 9 Johns. 253; Howell *v.* Ransom, 11 Paige, 538; De Rose *v.* Fay, 4 Edw. Ch. 40; Lewis *v.* J. A., Ibid. 599; Berrien *v.* McLane, 1 Hoffman, Ch. Rep. 424; Miles *v.* Ervin, 1 McCord, Ch. Rep. 524; Rose *v.* Mynell, 7 Yerger, 30; Bibb *v.* Smith, 1 Dana, 482; Smith *v.* Thompson's Heirs, 7 B. Monroe, 308; Jennings *v.* McConnel, 17 Illinois, 148.

An agreement made by a client with his counsel, after the latter had been employed in a particular business, by which the original contract is varied, and greater compensation is secured to the counsel than may have been agreed upon when first retained, is invalid and cannot be enforced. Lecatt *v.* Sallee, 3 Porter, 115.

phrases, fraud and presumption of fraud, as applied to him, may, and probably will, have an unfavorable effect on his reputation. Most emphatically should it be said, let nothing tempt him, not even the knowledge and consent of the client, to keep the money, which may have come to his hands professionally, one single instant longer than is absolutely necessary. The consequences of any difficulty arising upon this head, will be fatal to his professional character and prospects.

The official oath, to which reference has already more than once been made, obliges the attorney "to use no falsehood." It seems scarcely necessary to enforce this topic. Truth in all its simplicity—truth to the court, client, and adversary—should be indeed the polar star of the lawyer. The influence of only slight deviations from truth, upon professional character, is very observable. A man may as well be detected in a great as a little lie. A single discovery, among professional brethren, of a failure of truthfulness, makes a man the object of distrust, subjects him to constant mortification, and soon this want of confidence extends itself beyond the Bar to those who employ the Bar. That lawyer's case is truly pitiable, upon the escutcheon of whose honesty or truth, rests the slightest tarnish.

Let it be remembered and treasured in the heart of every student, that no man can ever be a truly great lawyer, who is not in every sense of the word, a good man. A lawyer, without the most sterling integrity, may shine for a while with meteoric splendor; but his light will soon go out in blackness of darkness. It is not in every man's power to rise to eminence by distinguished abilities. It is in every man's power, with few exceptions, to attain respectability, competence, and usefulness. The temptations which beset a young man in the outset of his professional life, especially if he is in absolute dependence upon business for his subsistence, are very great. The strictest principles of integrity and honor, are his only safety. Let him begin by swerving from truth or fairness, in small particulars, he will find his character gone—whispered away, before he knows it. Such an one may not indeed be irrecoverably lost; but it will be years before he will be able to regain a firm foothold. There is no profession, in which moral character is so soon fixed, as in that of the law; there is none in which it is subjected to severer scrutiny by the public. It is well, that it is so. The things we hold dearest on earth,—our fortunes, reputations, domestic peace, the future of those dearest to us, nay, our liberty and life itself, we confide to the integrity of our legal counsellors and advocates. Their character must be not only without a stain, but without suspicion. From the very commencement of a lawyer's career, let him cultivate, above all things, truth, simplicity, and candor: they are the cardinal virtues of a lawyer. Let him always seek to have a clear understanding of his object: be sure it is honest and right, and then march directly to it. The covert, indirect, and insidious way of doing anything, is always the wrong way. It gradually hardens the moral faculties, renders obtuse the perception of right and wrong in human actions, weighs everything in the balances of worldly policy, and ends most generally, in the practical adoption of the vile maxim, "that the end sanctifies the means." If it be true, as he has said, who, more than any mere man, before or since his day, understood the depths of human character, that one even may,

> "By telling of it,
> Make such a sinner of his memory;
> To credit his own lie:"—

we should be careful never to speak or act, without regard to the *morale* of our words or actions. A habit may and will grow to be a second nature.

> "That monster, custom, who all sense doth eat,
> Of habit's devil, is angel yet in this:
> That to the use of actions fair and good
> He likewise gives a frock or livery
> That aptly is put on."

There is no class of men among whom moral delinquency is more marked and disgraceful than among lawyers. Among merchants, so many honest men become involved through misfortune, that the rogue may hope to take shelter in the crowd, and be screened from observation. Not so the lawyer. If he continues to seek business, he must find his employment in lower and still lower grades; and will soon come to verify and illustrate the remark of Lord Bolingbroke, that "the profession of the law, in its nature the noblest and most beneficial to mankind, is in its abuse and abasement, the most sordid and pernicious."

While such are the depths to which a lawyer may sink, look, on the other hand, at the noble eminence of honor, usefulness, and virtue, to which he may rise. Where is the profession, which, in this world, holds out brighter rewards? Genius, indeed, will leave its mark in whatever sphere it may move. But learning, industry, and integrity, stand nowhere on safer or higher ground, than in the walks of the law. In all free countries, it is the avenue not only to wealth, but to political influence and distinction. In England, a large proportion of the house of peers, owe their seats and dignities, as well as their possessions, either to their own professional success, or to that of some one of their ancestors.* In this country, all our Presidents but three, have been educated to the Bar. Of the men who have distinguished themselves in the cabinet, in the halls of legislation, and in foreign diplomacy, how large is the proportion of lawyers! How powerful has always been the profession in guiding the popular mind, in forming that greatest of all counterchecks to bad laws and bad administration,—public opinion! It is the school of eloquence—that, which more than all else besides, has swayed, still sways, and always will sway, the destinies of free peoples. Let a man, to the possession of this noble faculty, add the high character of purity and justice, integrity and honor, and where are to be found the limits of his moral power over his fellow-citizens?† It is well to read

* In Foss's Grandeur of the Law, eighty-two existing peerages are stated to have sprung from the law. That was in 1843.

† Non merum, si ob hanc facultatem homines sæpe etiam

carefully and frequently, the biographies of eminent lawyers. It is good to rise from the perusal of the studies and labors, the trials and conflicts, the difficulties and triumphs, of such men, in the actual battle of life, with the secret feeling of dissatisfaction with ourselves. Such a sadness in the bosom of a young student, is like the tears of Thucydides, when he heard Herodotus read his history at the Olympic Games, and receive the plaudits of assembled Greece. It is the natural prelude to severer self-denial, to more assiduous study, to more self-sustaining confidence. Some one has recommended that Middleton's Life of Cicero should be perused, at frequent intervals, as the vivid picture of a truly great mind, in the midst of the most stirring scenes, ever intent upon its own cultivation and advancement, as its only true glory; and that in effect sketched by his own master hand.* The autobiography

non nobiles consulatum consecuti sunt: præsertim cum hæc eadem res plurimas gratias, firmissimas amicitias, maxima studia pariat. Cic. pro Muræna.

* Vivit, vivetque per omnium sæculorum memoriam.

of Edward Gibbon will rouse an ambitious student like the sound of a trumpet. But of English biographies, there is no one, it occurs to me, better adapted to the purpose mentioned, than the Life of Sir William Jones, by Lord Teignmouth. It exhibits the wonders, which unremitted study, upheld by the pure and noble ambition of doing good, can accomplish in the space of a short life. He was a man of the most varied knowledge. An extensive and indeed extraordinary acquaintance with ancient and modern languages, was perhaps his chief accomplishment. Although he engaged very late in life in the study of the law, such was his industry and success, that he soon occupied the highest judicial station, in British India; and the profession are indebted

Dumque hoc vel forte vel providentia vel utcunque constitutum rerum naturæ corpus, quod ille pæne solus Romanorum animo vidit, ingenio complexus est, eloquentia illuminavit, manebit incolume: comitem ævi sui laudem Ciceronis trahet; omnisque posteritas illius in te scripta mirabitur, tuum in eum factum execrabitur: citiusque in mundo genus hominum, quam cadet. Vell. Paterc. L. 2.

to his pen, for one of the most beautiful of the elementary treatises, which adorn the lawyer's library. "In his early days," says his biographer, "he seems to have entered upon his career of study, with this maxim strongly impressed upon his mind, that whatever had been attained, was attainable by him; and it has been remarked, that he never neglected nor overlooked any opportunity of improving his intellectual faculties, or of acquiring esteemed accomplishments." Notwithstanding his numerous occupations at the Bar at home, the onerous duties of his station in India, and his premature death, before he had attained his forty-eighth year, he has left behind many learned works, which illustrate Oriental languages and history, and attest the extent of his labors and acquisitions. Indeed, it might be regarded as impossible, were we not informed of the regular allotment which he made of his time to particular occupations, and his scrupulous adherence to the distribution he had thus made. The moral character of this eminent man, was no less exemplary. It is the testimony of one of his contemporaries: "He had more virtues and less faults, than I ever yet knew in any human being; and the goodness of his head, admirable as it was, was exceeded by that of his heart." His own measure of true greatness, humanly speaking, he has left behind him, in very emphatic words: "If I am asked, who is the greatest man? I answer, the best. And if I am required to say, who is the best? I reply, he that has deserved most of his fellow-creatures."*

This department of English literature has

* Sir William Jones adds to his other claims upon our admiration that of a decided partiality to the character and fortunes of our American Republics. "The sum of my opinion is," says he, "that while all the American people understand the modern art of war, and learn jurisprudence by serving in rotation upon grand and petit juries, their liberty is secure, and they will certainly flourish most when their public affairs are best administered by their Senate and Councils. I cannot think a monarchy or an oligarchy *stronger* in substance, whatever they may be in appearance, than a popular government. . . . . . . I shall not die in peace without visiting your United States for a few months before the close of the eighteenth century. May I find

been recently much enriched by the labors of the present Lord High Chancellor of England, Lord Campbell. In America we have a few well written and instructive legal biographies, among which ought especially to be named, Mr. Wheaton's Life of William Pinkney, and Professor Parsons' interesting Memoir of his distinguished father, Chief Justice Parsons. Mr. Binney, at the close of his honored and honorable life, is paying the debt, which every man owes to his profession, in animated spirit-stirring sketches of his great and good contemporaries. How forcibly does this distinguished jurist illustrate the remark of Cicero in his Treatise on Old Age: "Sed videtis, ut senectus non modo languida atque iners non sit, verum etiam sit operosa, et semper agens aliquid et moliens; tale scilicet, quod cujusque studium in superiore vita fuit." What a noble example might be held up, in the life

wisdom and goodness in your Senate, arms and judicature, which are power, in your commons, and the blessings of wealth and peace equally distributed among all." 2 Wynne's Eunomus, 359, note.

and character of Chief Justice Marshall! His biography, while it will be the record of active patriotism and humanity, will exhibit a course of arduous self-training, for the great conflicts of opinion, in which it was his lot afterwards to appear, with so much lustre. He had not the usual advantages of a collegiate education. The war of the Revolution, in which his ardent love of country, and of the principles of rational liberty, led him to enlist, and where he distinguished himself in the field, materially interfered with, and retarded his earlier professional studies; yet, the lofty eminence to which he attained in the opinion of his compatriots, even of those who could not concur in some of his views of the Constitution, the enduring monuments of his greatness in the decisions of the Supreme Court of the United States, bespeak an intellect of the very first order, mental power naturally vigorous, but brought, by proper exercise, to a degree of strength that made it tower above the general level of educated men. His opinions do not abound in displays of learning. His simplicity, a character so conspicuous in all his writings and actions—that first and highest characteristic of true greatness—led him to say and do just what was necessary and proper to the purpose in hand. Its reflected consequences on his own fame as a scholar, a statesman, or a jurist, seem never once to have occurred to him. As a judge, the Old World may be fairly challenged to produce his superior. His style is a model—simple and masculine. His reasoning—direct, cogent, demonstrative, advancing with a giant's pace and power, and yet withal so easy evidently to him, as to show clearly, a mind in the constant habit of such strong efforts. Though he filled for so many years the highest judicial position in this country, how much was his walk like the quiet and unobtrusive step of a private citizen, conscious of heavy responsibilities, and anxious to fulfil them; but unaware that the eyes of a nation —of many nations—were upon him! There was around him none of the glare, which dazzles; but he was clothed in that pure mellow light of declining evening, upon which we love to look. Where is the trust to society more sacred, where are duties more important, or consequences more extended, for individual or social weal or woe, than those which attach to the office he held? How apt, and aptly said, is that prayer of Wolsey, when he is informed of the promotion of Sir Thomas More to the place of Lord Chancellor:

> "May he . . . . do justice,
> For truth's sake and his conscience; that his bones,
> When he has run his course, and sleeps in blessings,
> May have a tomb of orphans' tears wept on him."

It is surely a just subject of national, as well as professional pride, that an American lawyer can thus, pointing to the example of such a man as JOHN MARSHALL, hold up his character, his reputation, his usefulness, his greatness, as incentives to high and honorable ambition; and especially, his life of unblemished virtue, and single-hearted purity,—after all, his highest praise, for, as old Shirley says,

> "When our souls shall leave this dwelling,
> The glory of one fair and virtuous action
> Is above all the scutcheons on our tomb."

Is it possible that a being so fearfully and wonderfully made as man, and animated by a spirit still more fearful and incomprehensible, was created for the brief term of a few revolutions of the planet he lives on? Shall his own physical and intellectual productions so long survive him? The massive piles of Egypt have endured for thousands of years: fluted column and sculptured architrave have stood for generations, monuments of his labor and skill. A poem of Homer, an oration of Demosthenes, an ode of Horace, a letter of Cicero, carry down to the remotest posterity the memorial of their names. Men found empires, establish constitutions, promulgate codes of laws; there have been Solons, Alexanders, Justinians, and Napoleons. There have been those justly called Fathers of their country, and benefactors of their race. Have they, too, sunk to become clods of the valley? The mind, which can look so far before and after—can subdue to its mastery the savages of the forests, and the fiercer elements of Nature—can stamp the creation of its genius upon the living canvas, or the almost breathing, speaking marble—can marshal the invisible vibrations of air into soul-stirring or soul-subduing music—can pour forth an eloquence of words, with magic power to lash the passions of many hearts into a raging whirlwind, or command them with a "peace, be still"—can make a book, a little book, which shall outlive pyramids and temples, cities and empires—can perceive and love beauty, in all its forms, and above all, moral beauty, and God, the infinite perfection of moral beauty,—no, this mind can never die. Its moral progress must go on in an unending existence, of which its life of fourscore years on earth is scarce the childhood. Let us beware then of raising these objects of ambition, wealth, learning, honor, and influence, worthy though they be, into an undue importance; nor in the too ardent pursuit of what are only means, lose sight of the great end of our being.

APPENDIX.

No. I.

COURVOISIER'S CASE.*

On Tuesday night, May 5th, 1840, Lord William Russell, infirm, deaf, and aged, being in his seventy-third year, was murdered in his bed. He was a widower, living at No. 14 Norfolk Street, Park Lane, London, a small house, occupied by only himself and three servants,—Courvoisier, a young Swiss valet, and two women, a cook and housemaid. The evidence was of a character to show very clearly that the crime had been committed by some one in the house; but, Courvoisier's behavior throughout had been that of an innocent man. Two examinations of his trunk, by the officers of the police, showed nothing suspicious; rewards having been offered by the government and family of the deceased, for the detection of the criminal, a third examination was made of Courvoisier's box, which

* Note at p. 47.

resulted in the discovery of a pair of white cotton gloves, two pocket handkerchiefs, and a shirt-front, stained with blood. The prisoner's counsel went to the trial with a full persuasion of his innocence, and conducted the cross-examination closely and zealously, especially of Sarah Mancer, one of the female domestics, with a view of showing that there was as much probability that the witness or the other domestic was the criminal as the prisoner; and that the police, incited by the hopes of the large rewards offered, had conspired to fasten the suspicion unjustly on him. At the close of the first day's proceedings, the prosecutors were placed unexpectedly in possession of a new and important item of evidence: the discovery of the plate of the deceased, which was missed, and that it had been left by the prisoner, at the place where it was found, about a week, perhaps only a very few days, before the committing of the murder. The parcel contained silver spoons, forks, a pair of gold auricles, all unquestionably the property of the unfortunate nobleman; and the only question remaining was, whether Courvoisier was the person who had so left it. If he were, it would, of course, grievously for him, increase the *probabilities* that it must have been he who subsequently committed the murder, and with the object of plunder. On the ensuing morning, the person who had made this discovery (Mrs. Piolaine, the wife of a Frenchman, who kept a place of entertainment, called L'Hotel de Dieppe, in Leicester Place, Leicester Square), was shown a number of prisoners in the prison-yard, one of whom was Courvoisier, whom she instantly recognized as the person who had left the plate with her, and also had formerly lived in her employ. Courvoisier also suddenly recognized her, and with dismay. The immediate effect of his panic was the confession of his guilt to his counsel at the bar of the court, a few minutes afterwards, coupled with his desire, nevertheless, to be defended to the utmost. His probable object was simply to prepare his counsel against the forthcoming evidence. The prisoner was convicted, and afterwards confessed his crime. Mr. Phillips's conduct of the defence was criticized at the time, in the columns of the Examiner, but he suffered it to pass in silence. In 1849, that periodical renewed the accusation originally made, upon which the following correspondence appeared in the London Times of Nov. 20th, 1849.

TO THE EDITOR OF THE "TIMES."

SIR,—I shall esteem it a great favor if you will allow the accompanying documents to appear in the "Times." Its universal circulation affords me an opportunity of annihilating a calumny recently revived, which has for nine years harassed my friends far more than myself.

I am, &c.,

CHARLES PHILLIPS.

39 Gordon Square.

INNER TEMPLE, Nov. 14, 1849.

MY DEAR PHILLIPS,—It was with pain that I heard yesterday of an accusation having been revived against you in the "Examiner" newspaper, respecting alleged dishonorable and most unconscientious conduct on your part, when defending Courvoisier against the charge of having murdered Lord William Russell. Considering that you fill a responsible judicial office, and have to leave behind you a name unsullied by any blot or stain, I think you ought to lose no time in offering, as I believe you can truly do, a public and peremptory contradiction to the allegations in question. The mere circumstances of your having been twice promoted to judicial office by two lord chancellors, Lord Lyndhurst and Lord Brougham, since the circulation of the reports to which I am alluding, and after those reports had been called to the attention of at least one of those noble and learned lords, is sufficient evidence of the groundlessness of such reports.

Some time ago I was dining with Lord Denman, when I mentioned to him the report in question. His lordship immediately stated that he had inquired into the matter, and found the charge to be utterly unfounded; that he had spoken on the subject to Mr. Baron Parke, who had sat on the Bench beside Chief Justice Tindal, who tried Courvoisier, and that Baron Parke told him he had, for reasons of his own, most carefully watched every word that you uttered, and assured Lord Denman that your address was perfectly unexceptionable, and that you made no such statements as were subsequently attributed to you.

Lord Denman told me that I was at liberty to mention this fact to any one; and expressed in noble and generous terms his concern at the existence of such serious and unfounded imputations upon your character and honor.

Both Lord Denman and Baron Parke are men of as nice a sense of honor and as high a degree of consciousness as it is possible to conceive; and I think the testimony of two such distinguished judges ought to be publicly known, to extinguish every kind of suspicion on the subject.

I write this letter to you spontaneously, and, hoping that you will forgive the earnestness with which I entreat you to act upon my suggestion, believe me ever yours sincerely,

SAMUEL WARREN.

MR. COMMISSIONER PHILLIPS.

39 GORDON SQUARE, NOV. 20.

MY DEAR WARREN,—Your truly kind letter induces me to break the contemptuous silence, with which for nine years I have treated the calumnies, to which you allude. I am the more induced to this by the representations of some valued friends, that many honorable minds begin to believe the slander because of its repetition without receiving a contradiction. It is with disgust and disdain, however, that even thus solicited I stoop to notice inventions too abominable, I had hoped, for any honest man to have believed. The conduct of Lord Denman is in every respect characteristic of his noble nature. Too just to condemn without proof, he investigates the facts, and defends the innocent. His deliberate opinion is valuable indeed, because proceeding from one who is invaluable himself. My judicial appointments by the noblemen you mention would have entailed on them a fearful responsibility, had there been any truth in the accusations of which they must have been cognizant. I had no interest whatever with either of these chancellors, save that derived from their knowledge of my character, and their observation of my conduct. It is now five-and-twenty years ago since Lord Lyndhurst, when I had no friend here, voluntarily tendered me his favor and his influence, and his kindness to me remains to this day unabated. Of Lord Brougham, my ever warm and devoted friend, I forbear to speak, because words cannot express my affection or my gratitude. His friendship has soothed some affliction and enhanced every pleasure, and while memory lasts will remain the proudest of its recollections and the most precious of its treasures. This is no vain-glorious vaunting. The unabated kindness of three of the greatest men, who ever adorned the Bench, ought, in itself, to be a sufficient answer to my traducers. Such men as these would scarcely have given their countenance to one, who, if what were said of him were true, deserved their condemnation. I am not disposed, however, though I might be well warranted in doing so, to shelter myself under the authority of names, no matter how illustrious. I give to each and all of these charges a solemn and indignant contradiction, and I will now proceed to their refutation. The charges are threefold, and I shall discuss them *seriatim.*

First, I am accused of having retained Courvoisier's brief after having heard his confession. It is right that I should relate the manner of that confession, as it has been somewhat misapprehended. Many suppose it was made to me alone, and made in the prison. I never was in the prison since I was called to the Bar, and but once before, being invited to see it by the then sheriffs. So strict is this rule, that the late Mr. Fauntleroy solicited a consultation there in vain with his other counsel and myself. It was on the second morning of the trial, just before the judges entered, that Courvoisier, standing publicly in front of the dock, solicited an interview with his counsel. My excellent friend and colleague, Mr. Clarkson, and myself immediately approached him. I beg of you to mark the presence of Mr. Clarkson, as it will become very material presently. Up to this morning I believed most firmly in his innocence, and so did many others as well as myself. "I have sent for you, gentlemen," said he, "to tell you I committed the murder!" When I could speak, which was not immediately, I said, "Of course then you are going to plead guilty?"—"No, sir," was the reply, "I expect you to defend me to the utmost." We returned to our seats. My position at this moment was, I believe, without parallel in the annals of the profession. I at once came to the resolution of abandoning the case, and so I told my colleague. He strongly and urgently remonstrated against it, but in vain. At last he suggested our obtaining the opinion of the learned judge, who was not trying the cause, upon what he considered to be the professional etiquette under circumstances so embarrassing. In this I very willingly acquiesced. We obtained an interview, and Mr. Baron Parke requested to know distinctly whether the prisoner insisted on my defending him, and, on hearing that he did, said, I was bound to do so, and to use all fair arguments arising on the evidence. I therefore retained the brief, and I contend for it, that every argument I used was a fair commentary on the evidence, though undoubtedly as strong as I could make them. I believe there is no difference of opinion now in the profession that this course was right. It was not until after eight hours' public exertion before the jury that the prisoner confessed; and to have abandoned him then would have been virtually surrendering him to death. This is my answer to the first charge.

I am accused, secondly, of having "appealed to Heaven as to my belief in Courvoisier's innocence," after he had made me acquainted with his guilt. A grievous accusation! But it is false as it is foul, and carries its own refutation on its face. It is with difficulty I restrain the expression of my indignation; but respect for my station forbids me to characterize this slander as it deserves. It will not bear one moment's analysis. It is an utter impossibility under the circumstances. What! appeal to Heaven for its testimony to a lie, and not expect to be answered by its lightning? What! make such an appeal, conscious that an honorable colleague sat beside me, whose valued friendship I must have forever forfeited? But above all and beyond all, and too monstrous for belief, would I have dared to utter that falsehood in the very presence of the judge to whom, but the day before, I had confided the reality! There, upon the Bench above me, sat that time-honored man—that upright magistrate, pure as his ermine, "narrowly watching" every word I said. Had I dared to make an appeal so horrible and so impious—had I dared so to outrage his nature and my own conscience, he would have started from his seat and withered me with a glance. No, Warren, I never made such an appeal; it is a malignant untruth, and sure I am, had the person who coined it but known what had previously occurred, he never would have uttered from his libel mint so very clumsy and self-proclaiming a counterfeit. So far for the verisimilitude of this charge. But I will not rest either on improbability, or argument, or even denial. I have a better and a conclusive answer. The trial terminated on Saturday evening. On Sunday I was shown in a newspaper the passage imputed to me. I took the paper to court on Monday, and, in the aldermen's room, before all assembled, after reading the paragraph aloud, I thus addressed the judges:—"I take the very first opportunity which offers, my lords, of most respectfully inquiring of you whether I ever used any such expression?"—"You certainly did not, Phillips," was the reply of the late lamented Lord Chief Justice, "and I will be your vouchee whenever you choose to call me."—"And I," said Mr. Baron Parke, happily still spared to us, "had a reason, which the Lord Chief Justice did not know, for watching you narrowly, and he will remember my saying to him, when you sat down, 'Brother Tindal, did you observe how carefully Phillips abstained from giving any personal opinion in the case?' To this the learned Chief Justice instantly assented." This is my answer to the second charge.

Thirdly, and lastly, I am accused of having endeavored to cast upon the female servants the guilt, which I knew was attributable to Courvoisier. You will observe, of course, that the gravamen of this consists in my having done so after the confession. The answer to this is obvious. Courvoisier did not confess till Friday: the cross-examination took place the day before, and so far, therefore, the accusation is disposed of. But it may be said I did so in my address to the jury. Before refuting this let me observe upon the disheartening circumstances under which that address was delivered. At the close of the, to me, most wretched day on which the confession was made, the prisoner sent me this astounding message by his solicitor: "Tell Mr. Phillips, my counsel, that I consider he has my life in his hands." My answer was, that as he must be present himself, he would have an opportunity of seeing whether I deserted him or not. I was to speak on the next morning. But what a night preceded it! Fevered and horror-stricken,

I could find no repose. If I slumbered for a moment, the murderer's form arose before me, scaring sleep away, now muttering his awful crime, and now shrieking to me to save his life! I did try to save it. I did everything to save it, except that which is imputed to me, but that I did not, and I will prove it. I have since pondered much upon this subject, and I am satisfied that my original impression was erroneous. I had no right to throw up my brief, and turn traitor to the wretch, wretch though he was, who had confided in me. The counsel for a prisoner has no option. The moment he accepts his brief, every faculty he possesses becomes his client's property. It is an implied contract between him and the man who trusts him. Out of the profession this may be a moot point; but it was asserted and acted on by two illustrious advocates of our own day, even to the confronting of a king, and, to the regal honor be it spoken, these dauntless men were afterwards promoted to the highest dignities.

You will ask me here whether I contend on this principle for the right of doing that of which I am accused, namely, casting the guilt upon the innocent? I do no such thing; and I deny the imputation altogether. You will still bear in mind what I have said before, that I scarcely could have dared to do so under the eye of Baron Parke and in the presence of Mr. Clarkson. To act so, I must have been insane. But to set this matter at rest, I have referred to my address as reported in the "Times"—a journal the fidelity of whose reports was never questioned. You will be amazed to hear that I not only did not do that of which I am accused, but that I did the very reverse. Fearing that, nervous and unstrung as I was, I might do any injustice in the course of a lengthened speech, by even an ambiguous expression, I find these words reported in the "Times,"—"Mr. Phillips said the prosecutors were bound to prove the guilt of the prisoner, not by inference, by reasoning, by such subtile and refined ingenuity as had been used, but by downright, clear, open, palpable demonstration. How did they seek to do this? What said Mr. Adolphus and his witness, Sarah Mancer? And here he would beg the jury not to suppose for a moment, in the course of the narrative with which he must trouble them, that he meant to cast the crime upon either of the female servants. It was not at all necessary to his case to do so. It was neither his interest, his duty, nor his policy, to do so. God forbid that any breath of his should send tainted into the world persons depending for their subsistence on their character." Surely this ought to be sufficient. I cannot allude, however, to this giant of the press, whose might can make or unmake a reputation, without gratefully acknowledging that it never lent its great circulation to these libels. It had too much justice. The "Morning Chronicle," the "Morning Herald," and the "Morning Post," the only journals to which I have access, fully corroborated the "Times," if, indeed, such a journal needed corroboration. The "Chronicle" runs thus:—"In the first place, says my friend Mr. Adolphus, and says his witness Sarah

Mancer—and here I beg to do an act of justice, and to assure you that I do not for a moment mean to suggest in the whole course of my narrative that this crime may have been committed by the female servants of the deceased nobleman." "The Morning Post" runs thus: "Mr. Adolphus called a witness, Sarah Mancer. But let me do myself justice, and others justice, by now stating, that in the whole course of my narrative with which I must trouble you, I beg you would not suppose that I am in the least degree seeking to cast the crime upon any of the witnesses. God forbid that any breath of mine should send persons depending on the public for subsistence into the world with a tainted character." I find the "Morning Herald" reporting me as follows: "Mr. Adolphus called a witness named Sarah Mancer. But let me do myself justice and others justice by now stating that in the whole course of the narrative with which I must trouble you, I must beg that you will not suppose that I am in the least degree seeking to cast blame upon any of the witnesses." Can any disclaimer be more complete? And yet, in the face of this, for nine successive years has this most unscrupulous of slanderers reiterated his charge. Not quite three weeks ago he recurs to it in these terms: "How much worse was the attempt of Mr. Phillips to throw the suspicion of the murder of Lord William Russell on the innocent female servants, in order to procure the acquittal of his client Courvoisier, of whose guilt he was cognizant?" I have read with care the whole report in the "Times" of that three hours' speech, and I do not find a passage to give this charge countenance. But surely, surely, in the agitated state in which I was, had even an ambiguous expression dropped from me, the above broad disclaimer would have been its efficient antidote.

Such is my answer to the last charge; and, come what will, it shall be my final answer. No envenomed reiteration, no popular delusion, no importunity of friendship, shall ever draw from me another syllable. I shall remain in future, as I have been heretofore, *auditor tantum.* You know well how strenuously and how repeatedly you pressed me to my vindication, especially after Lord Denman's important conversation with you, and you know the stern disdain with which I dissented. The *mens conscia recti*, a thorough contempt for my traducer, the belief that truth would in the end prevail, and a self-humiliation at stooping to a defence, amply sustained me amid the almost national outcry which calumny had created. Relying doubtless upon this, month after month, for nine successive years, my accuser has iterated and reiterated his libels in terms so gross, so vulgar, and so disgraceful, that my most valued friends thought it my duty to them publicly to refute them. To that consideration, and to that alone, I have yielded; in deference to theirs, relinquishing my own opinions. If they suppose, however, that slander, because answered, will be silenced, they will find themselves mistaken.

Destroy the web of sophistry—in vain—
The creature's at his dirty work again.

No, no, my dear friend, invention is a libeller's exhaustless capital, and refutation but supplies the food on which he lives. He may, however, pursue his vocation undisturbed by me. His libels and my answer are now before the world, and I leave them to the judgment of all honorable men.

C. Phillips.

No. II.

COURSE OF LEGAL STUDY.*

Non multa sed multum, is the cardinal maxim by which the student of law should be governed in his readings; at the commencement of his studies—in the office of his legal preceptor, Repetition—Repetition—Repetition. Blackstone and Kent, should be read—and read again and again. These elementary works, with some others of an immediately practical cast—Tidd's Practice, Stephen's Pleading, Greenleaf's Evidence, Leigh's Nisi Prius, Mitford's Equity Pleading—well conned, make up the best part of office reading. Of course the Acts of Assembly should be gone over and over again. I do not say that this is all. The plan of reading, which I am about to recommend,

* Note at p. 75.

may be begun in the office. Much will depend upon, what may be termed, the mental temperament of the student himself, which no one but the immediate preceptor can observe; and he will be governed accordingly in the selection of works to be placed in his hands. No lawyer does his duty, who does not frequently examine his student, not merely as a necessary means of exciting him to attention, and application; but in order to acquire such an acquaintance with the character of his pupil's mind—its quickness or slowness—its concentrativeness or discursiveness—as to be able to form a judgment whether he requires the curb or the spur. It is an inestimable advantage to a young man to have a judicious and experienced friend watching anxiously his progress, and able to direct him, when, if left to himself, he must wander in darkness and danger. "There be two things," says Lord Coke, "to be avoided by him as enemies to learning, *præpostera lectio* and *præpropera praxis.*" Co. Litt. 70 b.

I prefer presenting a certain order of subjects to be pursued; observing, however, that it may be somewhat irksome to pursue any one branch for too long a period unvaried. When that is found to be the case, the last five heads may be adopted as collateral studies, and pursued simultaneously with the first three.

These heads or branches are—1. Real Estate and Equity. 2. Practice, Pleading, and Evidence. 3. Crime and Forfeitures. 4. Natural and International law. 5. Constitutional Law. 6. Civil Law. 7. Persons and Personal Property. 8. The Law of Executors and Administrators.

I. Real Estate and Equity.

As introductory to this head, Lord Hale's History of the Common Law may be perused with advantage. It was perhaps a mere sketch, intended to be afterwards filled up and completed. Still, however, it is a work of authority, as indeed is everything which proceeded from the pen of its distinguished author. He is correct and accurate to a remarkable degree. Reeves' History of the English Law is a full and comprehensive history of the English Law, accurate and judicious as well as full. Lord Mansfield is said to have advised its author in regard to its plan and execution. In this work the student is presented with all that is necessary that he should know of the earliest law-books, Bracton, Glanville, and Fleta, carefully collected and presented. The history of the law is separately traced under the reign of each king, and it may be of advantage to read at the same time some good history or histories of England parallel with the work. "Reeves' History of the English Law," says Chancellor Kent, "contains the best account that we have of the progress of the law, from the time of the Saxons to the reign of Elizabeth. It covers the whole ground of the law included in the old abridgments, and it is a work deserving of the highest commendation. I am at a loss which most to admire, the full and accurate learning, which it contains, or the neat, perspicuous, and sometimes elegant style, in which that learning is conveyed." 1 Comm. 508.

Dalrymple's Essay towards a general History of Feudal Property in Great Britain, is a brief but learned and philosophical treatise, which may be followed by Sullivan's Lectures on Feudal Law, a work copious in detail and exhibiting ably, among other topics, the influence of the feudal system upon the Modern Law of Tenures. Sir Martin Wright's Introduction to the Law of Tenures is one of the most accurate and profound of the essays on this topic; and is worthy of the most attentive study. Craig de Feudis was thought by Lord Mansfield much preferable to any judicial work which England had then produced. With these legal treatises on the feudal system may be read with great advantage, simultaneously, Robertson's History of Charles V, and Hallam's History of the Middle Ages.

Sir Henry Finch's Law, or Nomotechnia, as he entitled it, may be taken up in this connection. It is said that until the publication of Blackstone's Commentaries, it was regarded as the best elementary book to be placed in the hands of law students; and we have the authority of Sir William Blackstone for saying that his method was greatly superior to that in all the treatises that were then extant: Blackstone's Analysis, Preface, 6. "His text," says Chancellor Kent, "was weighty, concise, and nervous, and his illustrations apposite, clear, and authentic;" though he adds, "But the abolition of the feudal tenures and the disuse of real actions, have rendered half of his work obsolete," 1 Comm. 509; an objection, in the view we take of legal education, which should rather recommend the work than otherwise.

At the same time with Finch take Doctor and Student by St. Germain—a little book which is replete with sound law, and has always been cited with approbation as an authority.

The Prefaces to the several volumes of Lord Coke's Reports may be read now with great advantage. They contain much interesting information, and strongly impregnated as they are with Lord Coke's abundant learning and love of the law as a science and profession, they form an admirable introduction to The First Institute, or Lord Coke's Commentary upon Littleton's Tenures. It would be advisable, I think, to read first in order the sections of Littleton's Tenures, the original treatise upon which The Institute was a commentary. After that, no time or pains should be spared to master completely The First Institute. If the course now prescribed has been followed, the student will not require to be reminded, that even those parts, which seem to relate to obsolete heads of the law, ought to be read and understood. "There is not," says Mr. Butler, "in the whole of this golden book, a single line which the student will not in his professional career, find on more than one occasion eminently useful." There may be some extravagance in this assertion; but we may nevertheless agree with Mr. Ritso that "there is no knowledge of this kind, which may not, sooner or later, be in fresh demand; there is no length of time or change of circumstances, that can entirely defeat its operation or destroy its intrinsic authority. Like the old specie withdrawn from circulation upon the introduction of a new coinage, it has always its inherent value; the ore is still sterling and may be moulded into modern currency." The opinions of American lawyers confirm this conclusion. It is well known that C. J. Parsons was distinguished for his familiarity with the pages of The Institute. It was Mr. Pinkney's favorite law book; and "his arguments at the Bar," says his biogapher, Mr. Wheaton, "abounded with perpetual recurrences to the principles and analysis drawn from this rich mine of common law learning." Mr. Hoffman, in his Course of Legal Study, has also borne his testimony to its importance to the American practitioner. Chancellor Kent seems, as I have intimated in the note, to lean rather against Coke upon Littleton, as an Institute of Legal Education, although he acknowledges its value and authority as a book of reference.

It appears to me that after Coke, Preston's Elementary Treatise on Estates may be read with advantage. He is perhaps unnecessarily diffuse and tautological; but he enters largely into the reasons of the abstruse doctrines of which he treats, and his work is calculated to lead the student to inquire more earnestly into the philosophy of the science. Fearne's Essay on the Learning of Contingent Remainders, should then be well studied. If no other book be read over a second time, it must not be omitted as to this. This volume is occupied in the discussion of points of great difficulty and abstruseness; yet the style is remarkable for clearness and perspicuity, and the reasoning is logical and irresistible. A taste or otherwise, for this book, will test the student's real progress. After Fearne, take up Sheppard's Touchstone of Common Assurances—a work generally supposed to have been written by Mr. Justice Doddridge, and not by William Sheppard, whose name it bears. It is a most valuable book, one of the most esteemed and authoritative of the old treatises. There is an edition by Mr. Preston, but I do not recommend it. Had he annotated in the common way, his labors and references would no doubt have increased the value of the book; but he has taken liberties with the text,—subdividing it, occasionally changing the phraseology, and inserting matter of his own: a course of proceeding in regard to any work, except a digest or dictionary, to which I cannot be reconciled. The Touchstone may be followed by Preston on Abstracts of Title, and Preston's Treatise on Conveyancing.

I think that at this period, as a necessary introduction to the succeeding studies, some works on Equity Jurisprudence should be taken in hand; as the Treatise on Equity of which Henry Ballow is the reputed author. It is the text of Fonblanque's Equity. It had better be read by itself. Disquisitional notes of great length only confuse and confound the student; and Mr. Marvin has well said that Fonblanque's Equity "finally expired under the weight of its own notes." To this add Jeremy's Treatise on Equity, and Story's Commentaries on Equity Jurisprudence. The student may then read with advantage, Powell on Mortgages, with Coventry's Notes. It is to be lamented that

Mr. Coventry did not prepare an original work, instead of overwhelming the text of Powell with his learned and valuable labors. Chancellor Kent has remarked, that between the English and American editors it is "somewhat difficult for the reader to know, without considerable difficulty, upon what ground he stands." Like the treatise on Equity, it has been nearly choked to death in the embraces of its annotators. Bacon's Reading upon the Statute of Uses, is a very profound treatise on that subject, though evidently left by its great author in an unfinished state. Sanders on Uses and Trusts, is a very comprehensive and learned work, and the subject, which may be styled the Metaphysics of the Law, requires close attention. Hill on Trustees, is a practical treatise, which may here be read with advantage, as also Lewis on Perpetuities. Sugden on Powers, has been said to be second to no elementary law book. It is a masterly elucidation of the subtle doctrines of the law on the subject of Powers, and is held in the highest estimation. It will perhaps be better appreciated and understood, if with it, or after it, is taken up Chance's Treatise on Powers,—a work more diffuse than Mr. Sugden's, and which examines, controverts, and discusses at large many of his positions. Sugden on Vendors and Purchasers may then follow.

The titles on Leases and Terms for Years, and Rent, in Bacon's Abridgment, should be studied. These were the works of Chief Baron Gilbert. After this, Woodfall on Landlord and Tenant.

Roscoe's Treatise on the Law of Actions relating to Real Property, may be read as a convenient introduction to Cruise on Fines and Recoveries, and Pigott on Common Recoveries.

To these, in conclusion of this, by far the most important and fundamental branch of legal studies, may be added, Powell's Essay on the Learning of Devises, and Jarman on Wills.

It will be remarked, that I have not set down in order, any Report Books; it is not that I undervalue that kind of study. It appears to me that in his regular reading, the student should constantly resort to and examine the principal cases referred to and commented upon by his authors. In this way, he will read them more intelligently, and they will be better impressed on his memory. Some reports may be read through continuously; such are Plowden, Hobart, Vernon, and I certainly think, Johnson's Chancery Reports should be thus read. Smith's Leading Cases is an excellent reading-book of this kind. The student of Pennsylvania Law will do well not to omit Binney's Reports. But I assign no particular place to this kind of study, because I think it may be taken up and laid aside at intervals, according to the bent of the student's inclination. When, in any particular part of his course, he finds his regular reading drags heavily—he has become fagged and tired of a particular subject—let him turn aside for a week or two, to some approved and standard Report Book; it will be useful reading, and he will be able to return refreshed to his proper course.

It would extend this Appendix too much, if I were to go over the remaining parts of the prescribed plan, with the same particularity as I have this first and most important branch. It will be sufficient to indicate merely the books, and the order in which they may be most profitably read, under each division.

II. Practice, Pleading, and Evidence.

The Introduction to Crompton's Practice gives a full account of the jurisdiction of the courts, and the steps by which it was arrived at. This book is sometimes called Sellon's Practice, having been arranged by Mr. Sellon. The fourth part of The Institutes of Lord Coke. Tidd's Practice. Stephen on Pleading. Saunders' Reports, with Notes by Williams. Broom's Parties to Actions. Greenleaf on Evidence. Selwyn's Nisi Prius. Leigh's Nisi Prius. Mitford's Pleading in Equity. Story's Equity Pleading. Barton's Historical Treatise of a Suit in Equity. Newland's Chancery Practice. Gresley on Evidence in Equity.

III. Crimes and Forfeitures.

Hale's History of the Pleas of the Crown. Foster's Crown Law. Yorke's Considerations on the Law of Forfeiture for High Treason. The third part of The Institutes of Lord Coke. Russell on Crimes and Misdemeanors. Chitty on Criminal Law.

IV. Natural and International Law.

Burlamaqui's Natural and Political Law. Grotius de Jure Belli et Pacis. Rutherford's Institutes. Vattel's Law of Nations. Bynkershoek Questiones Publici Juris. Wicquefort's Ambassador. Bynkershoek de Foro Legatorum. McIntosh's Discourse on the Study of the Law of Nature and Nations. Wheaton's History of International Law. Wheaton's International Law. Robinson's Admiralty Reports. Cases in the Supreme Court of the United States.

V. Constitutional Law.

The second part of Lord Coke's Institutes. Hallam's Constitutional History of England. Wynne's Eunomus. De Lolme on the English Constitution, with Stephens' Introduction and Notes. The Federalist. Rawle on the Constitution. Story on the Constitution. All the cases decided in the Supreme Court of the United States, on constitutional questions, to be read methodically, as far as possible.

VI. Civil Law.

I consider some study of this head as a necessary introduction to a thorough course on the subjects of Persons and Personal Property, and the topic, which is so important in the United States, of the Conflict of Laws.

Butler's Horæ Juridicæ. Gibbon's History of the Decline and Fall, chap. 44. Justinian's Institutes. Savigny's Traité de Droit Romain. Savigny's Histoire du Droit Romain au Moyen Age. Taylor's Elements of the Civil Law. Mackeldy's Compendium. Colquhoun's Summary of the Roman Civil Law. Domat's Civil Law.

VII. Persons and Personal Property.

Reeves on the Domestic Relations. Bingham's Law of Infancy and Coverture. Roper on Husband and Wife. Angel and Ames on Corporations. Les Œuvres de Pothier. Smith on Contracts. Story on Bailments. Jones on Bailments. Story on Partnership. Byles on Bills. Story on Promissory Notes. Abbott on Shipping. Duer on Insurance. Emerigon Traité des Assurances. Boulay-Paty Cour de Droit Commercial. Story on the Conflict of Laws.

VIII. Executors and Administrators.

Roper on Legacies. Toller on Executors. Williams on Executors. The Law's Disposal, by Lovelass.

I believe that the course that I have thus sketched, if steadily and laboriously pursued, will make a very thorough lawyer. There is certainly nothing in the plan beyond the reach of any young man, with ordinary industry and application, in a period of from five to seven years, with a considerable allowance for the interruptions of business and relaxation. One thing is certain,—there is no royal road to Law, any more than there is to Geometry. The fruits of study cannot be gathered without its toil. It seems the order of Providence that there should be nothing really valuable in the world not gained by labor, pain, care, or anxiety. In the law, a young man must be the architect of his own character, as well as of his own fortune. "The profession of the law," says Mr. Ritso, "is that, of all others, which imposes the most extensive obligations upon those who have had the confidence to make choice of it; and indeed there is no other path of life in which the unassumed superiority of individual merit is more conspicuously distinguished according to the respective abilities of the parties. The laurels that grow within these precincts are to be gathered with no vulgar hands; they resist the unhallowed grasp, like the golden branch with which the hero of the Æneid threw open the adamantine gates that led to Elysium."

No. III.

THE ENGLISH BAR.

There are three orders of men at the English Bar: 1. Attorneys, or Solicitors in Chancery. 2. Barristers; and 3. Serjeants.

1. *Attorneys and Solicitors.*—Acts of Parliament have been made for the regulation of this class. The Stat. 6 & 7 Vict. c. 73, consolidating and amending several of the laws relating to attorneys and solicitors, prescribes the conditions of admission as an attorney, the time and mode of their service under articles; and the oaths to be administered to them; and authorizes the Judges of the courts of the common law, and the Master of the Rolls to appoint examiners to examine the fitness and capacity of all persons applying to be admitted as attorneys or solicitors; and the certificate, either of the common law or equity examiners, will be sufficient to entitle a person so examined to admission in all the courts, examination by both not being necessary. 3 Stewart's Blackst. 29.

2. *Barristers.*—The proper legal denomination of this class is *apprentices*, being the first degree in the law conferred by the inns of court. Spelman defines apprentice, *tyro, discipulus, novitius in aliqua facultate.* This was probably the meaning of the term primarily; but as early

as the reign of Edward I, it was employed to denote counsel below the state and degree of serjeant at law; one degree corresponding to that of bachelor, and the other to that of doctor, in the universities (Pearce's History of the Inns of Court, 28). Lord Coke informs us, however, that this degree was anciently preferred to that of serjeant (2 Inst. 214). They were termed *apprenticii ad legem*, or *ad barras;* and hence arose the cognomen of *barristers*. A barrister must have kept twelve terms, *i. e.*, been three years a member of an inn of court, before he can be called to the Bar. After a member of an inn of court has kept twelve terms, he may, without being called, obtain permission to practice *under the Bar*. This class of practitioners are called *special pleaders* or *equity draftsmen* (according as they prepare pleadings in the common law or equity courts), or *conveyancers*, who prepare deeds. 3 Stewart's Blackst. 26, note. Those who are regularly called, however, may take upon them the causes of all suitors. Such of the barristers as have a patent of precedence, as king's counsel, sit within the Bar, with the serjeants; all others are called *utter* or *outer barristers*.

3. *Serjeants at law.—Servientes ad legem*, or serjeant-countors. The coif or covering to the head worn by this order has also given a denomination to them. There exists some differences of opinion among judicial antiquarians as to the origin of the coif. It is supposed by some to have been invented about the time of Henry III, for the purpose of concealing the clerical tonsure, and thus disguising

those renegade clerks, who were desirous of eluding the canon, restraining the clergy from practising as counsel in the secular courts. Hortensius, 349. By others it is referred to a much earlier period, when the practice in the higher courts was monopolized by the clergy, and those who were not in orders invented the coif to conceal the want of clerical tonsure. 1 Campbell's Lives of the Chief Justices, 85, note. There are, indeed, several circumstances to remind us of the ecclesiastical origin of our profession in England. The terms—on the festival of St. Hilary (Bishop of Poictiers, in France, who flourished in the fourth century); Easter; the Holy Trinity; and of the blessed Michael, the Archangel;—the habits of the judges, their appearance in court in scarlet, purple, or black, at particular seasons—the use of the word *brother* to denote serjeant, and *laity* to distinguish the people at large from the profession—the coif of the serjeants—the bands worn by judges, serjeants, and counsel, and the gown and hood of graduates of the inns of court,—many of such circumstances raise a strong presumption that the legal university was founded before the time of the enactment of the canons in the reign of King Henry III, compelling the clergy to abandon the practice of the law in the secular courts (Pearce's History, 22). *Nulles clericus nisi causidicus*, was the character given of the clergy, soon after the Conquest, by William of Malmsbury. The judges, therefore, were usually created out of the sacred order, as was likewise the case among the Normans; and all the inferior offices were supplied by the lower clergy, which has occasioned their successors to be styled *clerks* to this day (1 Bl. Com. 17). The livings in the gift of the Chancellor were originally intended as a provision for them, and an order was made in Parliament, 4 Edw. III, that "the Chancellor should give the livings in his gift, rated at twenty marks and under, to the King's clerks in Chancery, the Exchequer, and the two Benches, according to usage, and to none others." 1 Campbell's Lives of the Chancellors, 179, note.

In the time of Fortescue, sixteen years' continuance in the study of the law was the period of time considered a necessary qualification in candidates for the coif. There seems, however, never to have been a regulation to that effect; and it is certain that persons have often been advanced to this degree before that time. By the common law no one can be appointed a judge of the superior courts, who has not attained the degree of the coif; which degree can only be conferred on a barrister of one of the four inns of court. As soon as any member of an inn of court is raised by royal writ to the state, degree, and dignity of a serjeant-at-law, he ceases to be a member of the society. He removes to a new hall, and appears for the future in the inn of court as a guest (Pearce, 52).

The most valuable privilege formerly enjoyed by the serjeants (who, besides the judges, were limited to fifteen in number), was the monopoly of the practice in the Court of Common Pleas. A bill was introduced into Parliament in the year 1755, for the purpose of destroying this monopoly;

but it did not pass. In 1834, a warrant under the sign manual of the Crown was directed to the Judges of the Common Pleas, commanding them to open that court to the Bar at large, on the ground that it would tend to the general dispatch of business. This order was received, and the court acted accordingly. But in 1839 the matter was brought before the court by the serjeants, when it was decided that the order was illegal; Tindal, C. J., declaring that, "from time immemorial, the serjeants have enjoyed the exclusive privilege of practising, pleading, and audience in the Court of Common Pleas. Immemorial enjoyment is the most solid of all titles; and we think the warrant of the Crown can no more deprive the serjeant, who holds an immemorial office, of the benefits and privileges which belong to it, than it could alter the administration of the law within the court itself." (10 Bingh. 571; 6 Bingh. N. C. 187, 232, 235.) However, the Statute 9 & 10 Vict. c. 54, has since extended to all barristers the privileges of serjeants in the Court of Common Pleas.

www.ingramcontent.com/pod-product-compliance
Lightning Source LLC
LaVergne TN
LVHW011209110826
845150LV00006B/1371
* 9 7 8 1 4 2 5 5 1 7 5 1 9 *